Style Manual for Communication Studies

Third Edition

John Bourhis
Carey Adams
Missouri State University

Scott Titsworth
Ohio University

 **Higher Education**

Boston   Burr Ridge, IL   Dubuque, IA   New York   San Francisco   St. Louis
Bangkok   Bogotá   Caracas   Kuala Lumpur   Lisbon   London   Madrid   Mexico City
Milan   Montreal   New Delhi   Santiago   Seoul   Singapore   Sydney   Taipei   Toronto

Higher Education

Published by McGraw-Hill, an imprint of The McGraw-Hill Companies, Inc., 1221 Avenue of the Americas, New York, NY 10020. Copyright © 2009, 2006, 2002. All rights reserved. No part of this publication may be reproduced or distributed in any form or by any means, or stored in a database or retrieval system, without the prior written consent of The McGraw-Hill Companies, Inc., including, but not limited to, in any network or other electronic storage or transmission, or broadcast for distance learning.

This book is printed on acid-free paper.

1 2 3 4 5 6 7 8 9 0 DOC/DOC 0 9 8

ISBN: 978-0-07-338505-1
MHID: 0-07-338505-0

Editor in Chief: *Michael Ryan*
Publisher: *Frank Mortimer*
Sponsoring Editor: *Katie Stevens*
Development Editor: *Marley Magaziner*
Marketing Manager: *Leslie Oberhuber*
Production Editor: *Alison Meier*
Design Coordinator: *Ashley Bedell*
Cover Design: *Ashley Bedell*
Production Supervisor: *Tandra Jorgensen*
Composition: *10/12 Times Roman by ICC Macmillan Inc.*
Printing: *45# New Era Matte, R. R. Donnelley*

Library of Congress Cataloging-in-Publication Data

Bourhis, John.
   Style manual for communication studies / John Bourhis, Carey Adams, and Scott Titsworth. — 3rd ed.
      p. cm.
   Includes bibliographical references and index.
   ISBN-13: 978-0-07-338505-1 (alk. paper)
   ISBN-10: 0-07-338505-0 (alk. paper)
      1. Communication—Authorship—Style manuals. I. Adams, Carey.
   II. Titsworth, Scott. III. Title.
P96.A68S89 2009
808'.027—dc22

2008007089

The Internet addresses listed in the text were accurate at the time of publication. The inclusion of a Web site does not indicate an endorsement by the authors or McGraw-Hill, and McGraw-Hill does not guarantee the accuracy of the information presented at these sites.

www.mhhe.com

CONTENTS

PREFACE

The goal of this manual is simple yet ambitious. The *Style Manual for Communication Studies,* Third Edition, is designed to help reduce the number of errors made by students in their formal academic writing. It emerged out of our increasing frustration with our students' inability to communicate their thoughts and feelings effectively in written form. We might as well be speaking a foreign language when we mention *AP, APA, MLA,* or *Chicago Manual of Style.* We are convinced that either students are not receiving the instruction they need elsewhere or they forget most of what they are taught by the time they take courses in the discipline. Whatever the cause, the result is the same—most of our new graduate and undergraduate students do not know, understand, and/or use the rules for writing formal academic papers.

An extensive body of literature in our discipline indicates that the ability to communicate effectively in writing and orally will play a decisive role in the career success of our graduates. One of the authors can recall a student who, after receiving a failing grade on a written assignment because she had made 72 spelling, punctuation, grammatical, and format errors in a seven-page paper, responded, "I don't know why this writing stuff is so important. When I graduate I'll have a secretary who will do all this stuff for me!" More recently, one of the authors served on a university-wide committee that was responsible for selecting students to receive undergraduate university scholarships. An alarming number of very bright, highly motivated students, with otherwise impressive applications, did not receive support because they had made careless spelling, punctuation, and grammatical errors in putting together their applications. Spelling, punctuation, and grammar, as well as attention to detail and following conventions, do have real-world consequences.

The *Style Manual for Communication Studies* is designed to supplement whatever texts you currently use, in whatever courses you are currently taking or teaching. It contains condensed versions of the two most commonly used writing styles in our discipline (MLA and APA) and full-text examples written by graduate and undergraduate students. Because the conventions have been condensed to include only those most commonly needed, students will find this style guide more accessible and less intimidating. In this case, we believe less is more. If you intend to pursue advanced work in the discipline, we encourage you to purchase the complete copies of both the MLA and APA style manuals.

This edition of the *Style Manual for Communication Studies* contains the following features to help new graduate and undergraduate students write formal academic papers:

- Condensed versions of the most recent editions of the *Modern Language Association Handbook for Writers of Research Papers,* 6th ed. (New York, MLA, 2003) and the *Publication Manual of the American Psychological Association,* 5th ed. (Washington: APA, 2001).
- Current examples drawn from national and regional journals, leading texts and key works in the field of Communication Studies.
- Full-text examples of papers and preparation outlines written in MLA and APA-style documentation.
- Clear and concise rule boxes that highlight key conventions in both MLA and APA-style documentation.
- A revised and updated chapter devoted to critical evaluation and selection of supporting material, especially Internet-based sources.

We would like to thank our colleagues who have provided feedback and suggestions for improving the *Style Manual for Communication Studies,* including Frances Briggs, University of North Carolina Charlotte; Deborah J. Craig, Southwest Missouri State University; Kelli Munn, East Carolina University; Raymond R. Ozley, Washburn University. A special thank you to Matie Margavio Striley for her assistance with this revision.

John Bourhis, Carey Adams, and Scott Titsworth

CHAPTER ONE
LOCATING SOURCES OF
COMMUNICATION RESEARCH

Many writing assignments require you to locate and read primary source material, including reports of original research, critical reviews of past research, and theoretical essays. In addition to book-length publications, most primary source material is found in scholarly journals. This chapter provides information about journals that publish communication research, indexes you can use to search for information on specific topics, and Internet resources for investigating the communication discipline.

SCHOLARLY JOURNALS IN COMMUNICATION

Scholarly journals are very different from popular magazines (such as *Time* or *Newsweek*) and trade publications (such as *Advertising Age* or *Communication World*). One important difference is that scholarly journals are read primarily by scholars and professionals, as opposed to the general public or people with only a casual interest in the subject matter. A second important characteristic of scholarly journals is that they are more specialized than most popular periodicals. Scholarly journals often are dedicated to a particular discipline (such as communication or psychology), and may even be dedicated to particular areas of a discipline (for example, health communication or nonverbal communication). Third, popular periodicals and trade publications do not typically publish full-length reports of original research, whereas scholarly journals exist as an outlet for researchers and theorists to publish their original works.

Following are descriptions of selected scholarly journals that publish reports of original empirical and humanistic research, including their Library of Congress call numbers. (At the end of this chapter you'll find a more comprehensive list of communication-related journals that you may want to consult.) Note that some journals are considered "national" or "international" journals by virtue of their being published by national or international associations or having national and international circulations. Other journals are considered "regional" journals since they are published by regional associations, such as the Central States Communication Association, although many regional journals have national circulations. We have divided the journals by sponsor or other circulation characteristics.

We have included a list of commonly cited national and international journals. We have grouped the journal titles into four broad categories: International Communication Association journals, National Communication Association journals, Regional journals, and other commonly cited journals. Unless noted otherwise, these journals are all indexed in the *Communication and Mass Media*

Complete (CMMC) database as well as many other electronic databases common in the communication discipline and disciplines in the social sciences and humanities. Although most of these journals use the APA style manual to guide submissions, authors should consult a recent call for papers for specific requirements unique to the current editor.

INTERNATIONAL COMMUNICATION ASSOCIATION JOURNALS

Communication Theory (P87) is published quarterly and tends to include articles that address specific issues related to theory development, evaluation, and criticism. As such, many articles are critical essays rather than research reports, although some research reports that test certain elements of a theory may appear in the journal.

Communication Yearbook (P94.5.W65 W65x) is published annually and includes articles that explore topics in more depth than is typically available in journal-length submissions. The articles in *CY* tend to take the form of comprehensive, critical reviews and state-of-the-art essays.

Human Communication Research (P91.3 H85) is published quarterly and includes articles that reflect a behavioral and social scientific approach to studying communication. Most articles are quantitative in methodology, and many involve experiments. Other types of articles appearing in the journal could include discussions of methodology as well as philosophical essays on the study of communication.

The **Journal of Communication** (P90 .J6) is published quarterly and spans a wide variety of topics. The journal is intended as a general forum for communication scholarship and thus publishes articles related to all aspects of the discipline. An objective of the journal is to publish the "best available" scholarship on various issues.

The **Journal of Computer Mediated Communication** (TK5105.6 .J68) is a Web-based journal that publishes a broad range of manuscripts addressing the topic of computer mediated communication. The journal mainly publishes original, empirical research using social scientific methods. The journal is open access, which means that it is available free on the Web (http://jcmc.indiana.edu/).

NATIONAL COMMUNICATION ASSOCIATION (NCA) JOURNALS

Communication and Critical/Cultural Studies is published quarterly and features essays that cut across academic boundaries to study social, critical, and cultural practices from a communication perspective. The journal aims to promote critical reflection by addressing topics such as race, ethnicity, gender, ability, sexuality, and globalization.

Communication Currents is a relatively new online magazine published by NCA. Plans are for the magazine to be published quarterly on the *Communication Currents* Web site: http://www.communicationcurrents.com. NCA considers the publication to be a magazine because authors of scholarly articles appearing in other NCA journals summarize their manuscripts for lay readers in *Communication Currents*. The magazine is Web based and free through the Web site.

Communication Education (PN4071 .S74) is published quarterly and emphasizes articles exploring communication within classroom settings. Depending on the editor, the journal may focus on only general classroom/instructional communication topics or may also include articles related to communication pedagogy. Published articles include theoretical essays, critical reviews, empirical research reports, and other types of scholarly products.

Communication Monographs (PN4077 .S6) is published quarterly and is devoted mainly to the scientific and empirical investigation of communication processes. Work published in the journal must make a rational and compelling case for how the piece advances knowledge in a particular area.

Communication Teacher (PN4071 .S73) was formerly a quarterly print journal but now is published online. Articles can be accessed by NCA members or through CMMC. In addition, NCA members who subscribe to the journal receive a printed volume at the end of the year. The journal publishes articles describing original teaching activities relevant to the broad array of communication courses as well as manuscripts reporting the results of various types of communication assessment activities.

Critical Studies in Media Communication (P87 .C73) publishes quarterly and includes essays exploring media, audiences, representation, technologies, and professional practices. Most essays use a critical or cultural studies orientation. Manuscripts are required to be analytical and interpretive in nature rather than merely descriptive.

The **Journal of Applied Communication Research** (HM258 .J67) is published quarterly and includes articles that study communication in real-world situations. Results of such applied research are used to advance both theory and praxis to assist both scholars and practitioners in understanding how to address commonly occurring communication problems.

The **Journal of International and Intercultural Communication** is new for 2008. The journal includes articles relevant to an international community of scholars interested in intercultural communication using a broad range of methodological, conceptual, and theoretical perspectives. The aim of the journal is to focus on international, intercultural, and indigenous communication issues. The journal is indexed in CMMC and other databases.

The **Quarterly Journal of Speech** (PN4071 .Q2) is published quarterly and includes articles, research reports, and book reviews of interest to a broad range of readers in the communication arts. Essays published in the journal typically are humanistic in orientation and/or approach the study of communication from a humanistic, rhetorical, and/or cultural perspective. A variety of discourses are examined in the journal, ranging from traditional public addresses to mediated dialogue.

The **Review of Communication** publishes state-of-the-art reviews examining any sort of topic in the field. Such reviews might range from detailed book reviews to comprehensive reviews of literature on a topic of interest to the discipline. Four issues of the journal are published each year. This journal is available through CMMC but may not be indexed in conventional library catalogs.

Text and Performance Quarterly (PN2 .L69) is published quarterly and includes articles that explore and advance performance as a communicative act. Articles in the journal tend to be humanistic but approach the study of performance from a wide range of philosophical and theoretical traditions.

REGIONAL JOURNALS

Regional journals are published by one of the various regional communication associations. Although considered "regional," these journals have national circulation. The regional journals tend to be outlets for high-quality manuscripts that, for whatever reason, are not suited for national and international journals.

Communication Quarterly (PN4071 .T6) is a quarterly journal published by the Eastern Communication Association. The journal is "eclectically committed" to publishing high-quality research over a wide range of topics in the field, including research reports, critical reviews, theoretical essays, supported opinion papers, and other scholarly articles.

Communication Reports (P91.3 .C59) is published twice a year by the Western States Communication Association. The journal publishes brief reports of original data/text-based research using a variety of methods and perspectives.

Communication Research Reports (P87 .C59738x) publishes brief empirical research reports that are typically no longer than five to seven pages. Reports appearing in the journal pertain to a variety of topics including interpersonal, intercultural, small group, instructional, and computer-mediated communication, to name a few. The journal is published by the Eastern Communication Association.

Communication Studies (PN4001 .C45) is published quarterly by the Central States Communication Association. The journal publishes high-quality original scholarship exploring a variety of topics related to the communication process. This journal publishes articles using a variety of theoretical and methodological approaches.

Qualitative Research Reports in Communication (PN4071 .Q29) is an annual journal published by the Eastern Communication Association. The journal publishes brief critical essays and research reports that use qualitative/ interpretive methods to analyze a variety of topics in the field.

The **Southern Communication Journal** (PN4071 .S65) is published quarterly by the Southern Communication Association. The journal includes manuscripts that make significant contributions to our scholarly understanding of both the processes and consequences of communication. All methods and perspectives are welcomed by the journal.

The **Western Journal of Communication** (PN4071 .W45) is published quarterly by the Western States Communication Association. The journal publishes original scholarly manuscripts over a variety of topics in the field and welcomes all theoretical and methodological perspectives.

OTHER COMMONLY CITED JOURNALS

Communication Research (P951 .C56) is published six times per year by Sage Publications. Like journals published by academic organizations, manuscripts submitted to this journal undergo blind peer review. The journal publishes high-quality research on topics ranging from family communication and interpersonal communication to mass media.

Health Communication (R118) is published six times per year by Lawrence Erlbaum. The journal is designed as an outlet for scholarly discourse between medical and social sciences. The journal seeks to improve communication between stakeholders, medical professionals, patients, and other individuals involved in the health process.

The **Journal of Broadcasting and Electronic Media** (PN1991) is a quarterly journal published by the Broadcast Education Association. The journal contains articles about new developments, trends, and research in electronic media written by both academics and media professionals.

The **Journal of Family Communication** (HQ535) is published four times per year by Lawrence Erlbaum. The journal includes original research from all perspectives and methodologies related to the study of communication and the family.

The **Journal of Health Communication** (R118) is a scholarly, peer-reviewed journal published eight times per year by Taylor & Francis. The journal specializes in all forms of research related to a broad array of topics in health communication ranging from critical analyses of government policy to interpersonal and health campaign research in health settings.

Management Communication Quarterly (HD30.3) is published four times per year by Sage. The journal publishes rigorous, empirically supported, and practice-relevant research related to communication practices in a variety of management situations. The journal takes a cross-disciplinary approach and is targeted to both academics and practicing professionals.

Women's Studies in Communication (P94.5.W65 W65x) is published by the Organization for Research on Women and Communication, an affiliate organization of the Western States Communication Association. The journal is intended as a feminist forum for scholarship aimed at advancing our understanding of interrelationships between communication, gender, and feminism.

USING INDEXES TO LOCATE SOURCES IN COMMUNICATION

Scholarly journals are indexed and abstracted in a wide variety of publications and computerized databases. Many of these resources index journals across a wide variety of disciplines. For example, *Social Sciences Index* and *Humanities Index* will help you find material from many different fields. Most communication journals are included in these broad-based indexes. In addition, there are several indexes that are devoted entirely to communication studies, and these may be particularly useful to you if you are new to reading primary resource material in communication. The three most prominent communication indexes are *Communication Abstracts, Communication and Mass Media Complete,* and *Index to Journals in Communication Studies through 1990*. A detailed description of these three indexes is provided here, followed by brief descriptions of several other indexes and resources you may find useful in conducting your research.

Communication Abstracts was once a print-based reference tool but is now available online through *Cambridge Scientific Abstracts*. Your ability to access this database depends on whether your university subscribes to the Cambridge service. This index provides brief summaries, or abstracts, of the most recently published articles, books, and reviews related to communication, including speech communication, media, journalism, film, and other related areas. There are three ways to use *Communication Abstracts:*

1. Browse through the abstract entries until you find an article that appears interesting or relevant to you; then locate the article using the source citation given there.
2. Use the subject index to locate abstracts of publications on specific topics; then locate the article using the source citation.
3. Use the author index to locate articles by a specific researcher.

Each abstract contains several pieces of useful information. First, a complete bibliographic citation is provided so that you may locate the original source. Second, an abstract of approximately 150 words describes the purpose and contents of the source, including methods and results for research reports. Finally, a list of key terms by which the source is indexed is provided. For example, if one of the articles you found on persuasion was a study on the effectiveness of television commercials, key terms might include: advertising, brand recall, commercials, consumer behavior, perception, and television. You then could use these key terms to search for additional sources related to your specific topic.

Communication and Mass Media Complete is an electronic index available through many college and university libraries.The CMMC database provides citations from over 400 academic journals and trade magazines related to the discipline of communication. The database includes full-text articles for over 200 journals including most of the national journals in communication studies. You should ask your teacher or a reference librarian if your library subscribes to the CMMC database.

Using CMMC is no different from using other electronic databases or search engines. You may search using key words, the title of an article, subject terms, or the name of the author. You may also browse the table of contents of a particular journal indexed in the database.

Once you locate a particular article of interest, the database provides you with complete bibliographic information for the article and an abstract summarizing the article's content. If the article comes from a journal with full-text coverage, you will see a link to download the article.

Communication research is indexed in a variety of other sources, including indexes of scholarship in other disciplines related to communication. Here is a brief listing of printed and computerized indexes that you may find useful.

- *Business Education Index* (1940 C), indexes materials related to business.
- *Business Periodicals Index* (1958 C), indexes all categories of business journals.

- *Communication Abstracts* (1991 C), see above.
- *Current Contents: Social and Behavioral Sciences* (1974 C), reproduces tables of contents for 1,300 journals and articles from edited books.
- *Current Index to Journals in Education* (1969 C), indexes contents of education journals.
- *Dissertation Abstracts* (1966 C), abstracts doctoral dissertations in the United States and Canada.
- *ERIC* (1966 C), is a CD-ROM index combining the *Current Index to Journals in Education* and *Resources in Education*. Many unpublished papers presented at academic and professional conferences are available through *ERIC*.
- *Humanities Index* (1974 C), indexes over 340 English-language periodicals in the humanities.
- *IAC Business Index* (1990 C), indexes over 900 journals and business newspapers with citations concentrated in the field of business.
- *IAC Expanded Academic Index* (1990 C), indexes over 1,500 journals, including many in communication as well as other social sciences and humanities.
- *PAIS Bulletin* (1915 C 1990), indexes books, periodicals, and documents on contemporary public issues. Continued as *PAIS International in Print.*
- *Psychological Abstracts* (1927 C), indexes and abstracts sources related to the field of psychology.
- *Psyclit* (1974 C), is a CD-ROM version of *Psychological Abstracts.*
- *Resources in Education* (*RIE*) (1966 C), indexes research in education, most of which is not published elsewhere.
- *Social Sciences Index* (1974 C), indexes over 350 English-language periodicals related to the social sciences.
- *Sociological Abstracts* (1953 C), indexes and abstracts sources related to the discipline of sociology.
- *Sociofile* (1974 C), is a CD-ROM version of *Sociological Abstracts.*

SEARCHING, SURFING, AND BROWSING: USING ONLINE RESOURCES

Indexes are useful for locating published sources on particular topics, but there are even more timely ways of keeping up to date on the latest developments in various fields. A large variety of online bulletin boards, LISTSERV user groups, Web sites, and electronic publications are available to you via computer. By accessing these sources you can "listen in" on current debates among scholars and experts, or even participate yourself! You can also locate information and resources not available anywhere in print. Following is a brief listing of several online sources you may find helpful and interesting. There are many more, and more are being added every day. Most sites on the Web also have built-in links to other related sites. Following these links is an easy way to explore sites related to your interests.

The **American Communication Association** is a national organization of communication scholars and professionals from across the discipline. Its Web site includes extensive resources, including bibliographies, interest groups, an index of online books and texts, and a wide array of links to related sites. Contact the ACA Web site at http://www.americancomm.org/

The **Applied and Organizational Communication Network** is a LISTSERV discussion group with participants primarily from the fields of management and communication (app-orgcom@creighton.edu; subscribe by sending a message to majordomo@creighton.edu)

The **Center for Electronic Texts in the Humanities** includes an inventory of electronic texts in the humanities, including more than 75 journals, and access to collections of electronic texts: http://www.ceth.rutgers.edu

The **Communication Research and Theory Network (CRTNET)** is a LISTSERV discussion group maintained by the National Communication Association. Participants post notices ranging from discussions of theoretical and practical issues to announcements of conferences. Transcripts of major political speeches, such as the President's State of the Union Address or presidential campaign speeches, are also routinely posted on CRTNET. Participation in CRTNET is free. To subscribe, point your browser to http://lists1.cac.psu.edu/cgi-bin/wa?A0=CRTNET

CIOS/Comserve is an online service of the Communication Institute for Online Scholarship. Comserve provides access to a resource library of scholarly papers, research materials, bibliographies, syllabi, archives of online discussions, and newsletters, as well as interest group hotlines and *The Electronic Journal of Communication/La Revue Electronique de Communication.* Some of Comserve's services are free, while others are reserved for those who pay an individual membership fee or departments that are institutional affiliates. Your institution's library may have a subscription that will allow you to access these services. Two particularly useful member services are Com Abstracts, a database of abstracts in the professional literature, and Com Web Mega Search, a full-text index of over 12,000 publication titles in the field of communication. For more information about Comserve, send an e-mail message to Comserve@cios.org. There is also a Comserve Web site: http://www.cios.org

The **International Communication Association** is a major international association for academics and professionals in many areas of communication. On their Web site, you will find information about ICA, listings of conference programs, bibliographies, and links to other related sites: http://www.icahdq.org/

Scholarly Journals Distributed via the World Wide Web, maintained by the University of Houston Libraries, provides information about online

scholarly journals in a variety of disciplines: http://info.lib.uh.edu/wj/
webjour.htm

The **National Communication Association,** one of the major associations for
academics and professionals in the field of communication, maintains a Web site
that includes information about upcoming conferences, NCA members, and even
job placement: http://www.natcom.org/

Uncover Reveal is a unique service that will automatically e-mail you the table
of contents of a large variety of scholarly journals. Contact Uncover Reveal by
sending a Telnet message to database.carl.org and following the instructions.

A REPRESENTATIVE LIST OF
SCHOLARLY COMMUNICATION JOURNALS

- *American Speech*
- *Argument Studies Quarterly*
- *Association for Communication Administration Bulletin*
- *Basic Communication Course Annual*
- *Broadcasting*
- *Business Communication Quarterly*
- *Cinema Journal*
- *Communication*
- *Communication and Cognition*
- *Communication and the Law*
- *Communication Education*
- *Communication Monographs*
- *Communication Quarterly*
- *Communication Research: An International Quarterly*
- *Communication Research Reports*
- *Communication Studies*
- *Communication Theory*
- *Communication Yearbook*
- *Critical Studies in Media Communication*
- *Educational Communication and Technology*
- *European Journal of Communication*
- *Film Comment*
- *Film Journal*
- *Health Communication Research*
- *Howard Journal of Communications*
- *Human Communication Research*
- *Information and Behavior*
- *International Journal of Advertising*
- *International Journal of American Linguistics*
- *Journal of Applied Communication Research*

- *Journal of Broadcasting and Electronic Media*
- *Journal of Business Communication*
- *Journal of Business and Technical Communication*
- *Journal of Communication*
- *Journal of Language and Social Interaction*
- *Journal of Popular Film*
- *Journal of the University Film Association*
- *Journalism Quarterly*
- *Language*
- *Language and Communication*
- *Language and Social Psychology*
- *Language and Speech*
- *Linguistics*
- *Management Communication Quarterly*
- *Marketing and Media Decisions*
- *Mass Communication Review*
- *Media and Methods*
- *Media and Values*
- *Media Culture and Society*
- *National Forensic Journal*
- *Philosophy and Rhetoric*
- *Political Communication and Persuasion*
- *Quarterly Journal of Speech*
- *Quarterly Review of Film Studies*
- *Rhetoric Society Quarterly*
- *Southern Communication Journal*
- *Telecommunication Journal*
- *Text and Performance Quarterly*
- *Western Journal of Speech Communication*
- *Women's Studies in Communication*
- *World Communication*

CHAPTER TWO
CHOOSING SUPPORTING MATERIAL WISELY

This chapter focuses on subjective elements of effective writing and speaking. Specifically, you will learn about the decision-making process involved in carefully selecting supporting materials for a paper or speech outline. In this chapter we identify several guidelines, or "rules of thumb," for selecting and using support material. We begin with a discussion of why it is necessary to critically evaluate sources of information. Next, we identify guidelines for evaluating support material used in a speaking outline or research paper. Finally, we identify common errors related to the use of supporting material that we have encountered in student research papers, essays, and speeches.

THE ETHICAL AND PRAGMATIC NECESSITY OF SOURCE EVALUATION

Contemporary writers and speakers are faced with a double-edged sword created by the exponential growth of information. Although it is easier than ever to find supporting material, determining what supporting materials should be included in a well-developed manuscript or speech is more difficult. Whether you are composing a speech or writing a research report, you are developing arguments using information from external sources. For that reason, supporting material may be viewed as building blocks for your arguments. Authors must make subjective decisions concerning the use of supporting material so that their arguments make the strongest possible case for their conclusion. More specifically, writers are justified in critically evaluating sources for two reasons: First, there is a pragmatic necessity to limit the amount of supporting material included in a speech or paper. Second, there is an ethical responsibility to only include supporting material that is accurate and appropriate. We briefly expand on both of these points before turning to criteria used for evaluating sources.

Anyone using the Internet to conduct research has encountered frustration when searching for a specific source using one of the popular search engines like Google or Yahoo. These search tools return hundreds or thousands of possible sources, and you are left with the options of painstakingly reviewing each source, randomly checking sources that look remotely relevant, or simply giving up. Unfortunately, your difficulty does not end there. For any given topic there may be hundreds of research articles, books, government documents, and popular press articles that could also be relevant. Thus, you are faced with the overwhelming task of sifting through a seemingly endless list of possible references. Because of time constraints and length limitations, one cannot possibly review and include every possible source on a given topic. For that pragmatic reason alone, careful evaluation of sources is critical.

In addition to the strong pragmatic reasons for evaluating sources, there are also compelling ethical reasons why you must be selective about the use of supporting material. Writers and speakers alike are reminded that they have an ethical obligation to their audience. In our opinion, this is the single most important guideline that guides research. The author of a speech or manuscript acts as a gatekeeper who presents a filtered view of information to audience members, and, in many cases, the audience will base its understanding of the information on what the author presents. For that reason, you must ensure that the audience can make an informed decision about the information presented. The guidelines we present in the next section were selected because they are based, in part, on your ethical responsibility to the audience.

FIVE GENERAL GUIDELINES FOR EVALUATING SOURCES

When researching a topic it is often necessary to develop a screening process for supporting material. In this section we present five guidelines that speakers and writers may use to evaluate potential sources of information.

IS THE SUPPORTING MATERIAL CLEAR?

Supporting material may be used for a variety of purposes in a manuscript or speech; not the least of which is to add clarity to arguments being presented. If supporting material is difficult to explain, filled with technical jargon, or requires extensive background information, it may be useless for the purpose at hand to create a clear speech or well-explained paper.

IS THE SUPPORTING MATERIAL VERIFIABLE?

Recall that the primary function of correct source citation, whether it be in APA or MLA style, is to aid readers who are interested in finding additional information or verifying the sources used in the manuscript. Thus, a second guideline for evaluating the usefulness of supporting material is the extent to which the material is verifiable.

When grading various writing assignments and public speeches, we have often encountered students using personal interviews with roommates, friends, and even "people on the street" as supporting material. Although these sources can, in some cases, help make topics more concrete for audience members or readers, these sources are often difficult to verify. The same problem can occur when using personal e-mail and even Internet documents. Since Web pages can be updated several times a day it may be impossible to verify what was on a particular Web page when the initial research was gathered. Authors are encouraged to avoid using unverifiable supporting material when making important claims in their manuscripts or speeches. If using such evidence for anecdotal purposes, additional evidence from verifiable sources is warranted.

IS THE SOURCE OF THE SUPPORTING MATERIAL COMPETENT?

Source qualification is an often overlooked component of supporting material. Put simply, source competence assumes the source of the supporting material has some experience or expertise with the topic in question. Without such qualifications, the conclusions drawn from a source may amount to nothing more than uneducated guesswork. In public speaking, the issue of source competence typically includes analysis of the following questions:

- Does the source have significant experience with the topic in question?
- Is the source considered an authority in the field?
- Has the source conducted original research on the topic?
- Is the source well respected?

For academic writing, there are additional criteria relevant to the competence of sources. Most teachers prefer that students use primary rather than secondary sources in their papers. Secondary sources summarize original research. For example, a textbook on interpersonal communication summarizes research on several topics related to interpersonal communication in a variety of contexts. Although the summaries of research in the interpersonal text are likely accurate and well written, they are merely reinterpretations of original research similar to an encyclopedia entry. Primary sources, on the other hand, are original published works. For example, a research article reporting the results of a qualitative research study on interpersonal deception would be considered primary. Most teachers prefer that students use secondary sources only as a way of locating primary sources. For instance, you might use the references cited in your interpersonal communication text as a starting point for finding primary sources on interpersonal deception theory.

In addition to using sources from respected academic journals, writers must also consider the credibility of individual authors on a given topic. Fortunately, writers of research papers are not required to place the same emphasis as required of public speakers on identifying source qualifications. Because manuscripts have bibliographies, readers can easily investigate the qualifications of particular sources if they so wish. However, the fact that a manuscript may not contain source qualifications does not absolve authors from recognizing the importance of this criterion. For any given research topic there are likely seminal books and articles that should be cited when explaining the concept. For instance, almost every literature review and scholarly article on communication apprehension cites James McCroskey's definition of the concept. Indeed, one may question the legitimacy of a manuscript that does not cite classic works in the area being addressed. By using a combination of secondary and primary sources, it is relatively easy to identify key sources that should be consulted and reviewed on any particular communication topic.

IS THE SOURCE OF THE SUPPORTING MATERIAL OBJECTIVE?

Related to source competence is the question of whether or not the source is biased or predisposed to take a certain position on the topic in question. Consider the current national debate regarding violence in schools. On this particular issue, a speaker should be skeptical of supporting material obtained from the National Rifle Association. Clearly, this organization and its representatives have a very strong motive for advocating a particular viewpoint on this issue.

Although bias is self-evident on a controversial topic like gun control, writers must be aware that biases can exist on any given issue: A researcher may have a bias toward a particular theoretical perspective or research methodology; a book author may have a bias toward a particular political ideology; even friends may have a bias influencing their viewpoint on an issue. When using any source it is important to question whether individual biases cloud the source's judgment on an issue to such a degree that his or her conclusions are not sound. Moreover, authors have an ethical responsibility to point out potential biases when presenting supporting material to readers and audience members.

IS THE SUPPORTING MATERIAL RELEVANT?

The final general guideline questions whether or not supporting material is relevant to the topic in question. It seems self-evident that one should not include irrelevant supporting material. However, students often perceive an advantage to using the "shotgun" approach for researching a topic. That is, instead of focusing research efforts on key arguments, inexperienced writers often include easy-to-find supporting material that is of marginal relevance. Although this approach can give the appearance of a well-documented speech or paper, careful readers and listeners can see through this tactic. As a general rule, it is wise to include a few quality sources and explain those sources well rather than including several sources that are minimally explained and have little relevance to the specific issue being addressed.

In summary, writers and speakers have an ethical responsibility to ensure that the supporting material they use is accurate, objective, and relevant to their topics. When choosing between various supporting materials, there are several guidelines you can use to assess quality. Recall that these guidelines are relevant for any project involving research, whether it be a speech or research paper.

> **What guidelines should be used for evaluating the quality of source material used in my writing and speaking?**
>
> 1. Is the supporting material clear (clarity)?
> 2. Is the supporting material verifiable (verifiability)?
> 3. Is the source of the supporting material competent (competence)?
> 4. Is the source of the supporting material objective (objectivity)?
> 5. Is the supporting material relevant (relevance)?

APPLYING EVALUATION GUIDELINES TO INTERNET SOURCES

The Internet has transformed the way research is conducted. In our opinion, students are too dependent on supporting material gained from the Internet. Although the trend toward using the Internet as a primary research tool is not surprising, it is alarming. Our position is direct: Many Internet sources are of poor quality and, consequently, are inappropriate for use in formal academic writing and effective public speaking. In addition, students are not being adequately trained to make meaningful distinctions between sources of supporting material that are credible and appropriate versus those that are deceptive, unreliable, and potentially harmful to others.

As discussed earlier, the advantage offered by the Internet is often counteracted when writers do not discriminate among sources. Put simply, not all sources of information are good. Effective speakers and writers must learn steps necessary for distinguishing among sources quickly. This section illustrates how several of the previously discussed guidelines may be applied to Internet sources. We pay particular attention to the issue of source credibility and qualifications and explain steps necessary for determining the source of Internet pages.

For this example, we conducted an Internet search for information on interpersonal communication. Using Google, we found just under 3 million Web pages relevant to the phrase "interpersonal communication." We highlight only four of the returned sites to illustrate how to apply some of the guidelines mentioned in the previous section. These descriptions are exactly as they appeared in the search results.

Interpersonal Communication – Wikipedia, the Free Encyclopedia
Interpersonal communication is the subject of a number of disciplines in the field of psychology, notably Transactional analysis. . . .
en.wikipedia.org/wiki/Interpersonal_communication - 27k –

Four Principles of Interpersonal Communication
These principles underlie the workings in real life of interpersonal communication. They are basic to communication. We can't ignore them . . . www.pstcc.edu/facstaff/dking/interpr.htm - 5k -

Interpersonal Communication
Interpersonal Communication "Work by Canary and Stafford (1992) identifies five maintenance strategies (many associated with ways to manage conversations) that have proved most successful in long-term relationships: positivity, openness, assurances, networks, and sharing tasks." (Tubbs & Moss, Human Communication, p. 189) http://www.mhhe.com/socscience/speech/commcentral/mginterper . . .

Interpersonal Communication Articles
Interpersonal Communication articles written by a diverse group of experts, speakers, professionals, consultants, and marketing companies. The information within these articles will speed the growth of any small and home based business. http://www.pertinent.com/pertinfo/business/communication/

Results for this search include a title for the Web site and additional information, including a brief description of the site, and the Internet address. Most search engines include an option to return summaries and other information with search results; however, this option may need to be selected. As you become more familiar with conducting research on the Internet, it is easier to explore search results quickly. More importantly, experience using the Internet can help you become more effective at screening potential information to find the best sources available on a topic.

Several of the strategies discussed previously in this chapter may be used to assess the quality of Internet sources. Just by examining summaries of Web sites, we can quickly assess the quality of potential sources in terms of how relevant they are to the topic in question and the credibility of the source. For instance, the first Web site is Wikipedia, the free online encyclopedia. Most teachers and serious researchers are highly skeptical of Wikipedia because anyone can write and update the articles contained in the encyclopedia. Whereas some information might be correct, the quality control of such a service is questionable at best. The last source is a ".com" source and, consequently, is not scholarly in nature. The second of the sources is from a professor's Web site, but still deserves some scrutiny because most academic sites do not have any sort of editorial review. The point we are making is this: All Web sites found through Google and other search engines deserve careful scrutiny. Remember, Google is "free," and higher quality information will likely come from a fee-based service through a library or other trusted source.

Basic knowledge of Internet addresses can help you determine what type of organization created the Web page, and you can avoid wasting time reviewing the home page of a source. In general, Internet addresses follow this format:

Protocol://document-type.server.suffix/directory/file.name

The protocol and document type are typically the "http://" and "www" designations. The server is simply the name of the actual computer where the Internet page is located. In particular, researchers should pay attention to the suffix of the Web site. Five of the most common suffixes are .edu (education), .org (organization), .com (commercial), .gov (government), and .net (network). The Internet address may contain an additional suffix if the server is from a country other than the United States. For instance, a document housed on an Australian server has the suffix ".au" after the primary suffix.

Although this is a generalization, education servers and government servers may be more relevant for academic research than commercial and network servers. Organization servers may be appropriate for use if the organization is a recognizable not-for-profit organization like the American Red Cross or the National Communication Association. Researchers should understand that Internet addresses can be obtained easily and, consequently, should be used as only one potential indicator of a particular source's quality. For instance, most students and faculty can easily obtain university accounts and publish Web pages with an ".edu" suffix; however, those Web pages may not be reliable for academic research. In our example, the "Interpersonal Communication" site is from a commercial server; however, it is from a textbook publisher and would be of much higher quality than other commercial sites. The point is, pay attention to the type of server but do not assume that all of one type of domain is "bad" or that another is "good."

Once sites are selected for possible inclusion in a manuscript or speech, what other information might a researcher need to obtain before determining whether or not to use a particular source? Initially, authors should review each site to determine whether a source is identified, when the site was last updated, and what the purpose of the site is. For instance, the return address for the "Interpersonal Communication" page is for a particular file and not the main page for that Web site. To find out relevant information about this site, it is necessary to scroll down to learn that the site is part of McGraw-Hill's communication Web site. In other cases, it may be necessary to backtrack and find the index page for a particular site to obtain this information. Once this information is obtained, the researcher can determine the credibility and biases of the source.

Once all of this information has been reviewed, researchers should evaluate the ideas contained in a Web document as if it were a journal article, book, or magazine. In particular, the researcher may apply several of the guidelines described previously. In light of the possible evidence for a particular issue, do the Web pages clearly explain and illustrate the concept? Is the author, either a person or an organization, competent and bias free? Is it possible to verify conclusions drawn by the sources? In particular, we stress the fact that information obtained via the Internet must be verifiable. Recall that verification requires that sources and arguments can be confirmed. To apply this principle, we adhere to the independent confirmation standard. The independent confirmation standard simply requires that before using any material, one should first find other sources making the same claims, observations, or drawing the same conclusions. By obtaining independent confirmation, one is fulfilling ethical responsibilities toward the audience by ensuring that information contained in a manuscript or speech is accurate. For our topic of interpersonal

> The independent confirmation standard simply requires that before using any material, one should first find other sources making the same claims, observations, or drawing the same conclusions. By obtaining independent confirmation, one is fulfilling ethical responsibilities toward the audience by ensuring that information contained in a manuscript or speech is accurate.

communication, we might seek independent confirmation by consulting volumes of *Communication Monographs, Communication Yearbook,* or one of the several textbooks on this issue. Effective researchers make use of a variety of different sources of supporting material, including traditional resources found in a library.

FINAL THOUGHTS ON CHOOSING SUPPORTING MATERIAL WISELY

In this chapter we have provided several suggestions for researching and evaluating support material. Specifically, we identified five general criteria for evaluating sources and addressed the specific issue of using the Internet to conduct research, stressing that many Web pages are simply inappropriate to use in speeches and papers. It is wise to independently confirm any information obtained on a Web page.

After you have reviewed this information, it should be clear to you that good research involves much more than simply compiling a list of sources. Good research involves systematic evaluation of sources to find the best possible supporting material for arguments being made in a manuscript or speech. We conclude our discussion of evaluating supporting material by pointing out many of the common errors we see students make in speeches and papers.

- Internet addresses for Web sites should not be cited as the "source" of a Web site. They are addresses, not sources. Instead, the author, editor, Webmaster, or sponsoring organization should be cited as the "source." The Internet address is analogous to the title of a journal and, therefore, should only be included in the bibliography. It would be like providing the address for your school library as the "source" of supporting material found in a journal! Imagine how silly you would sound, "According to 901 South National Avenue in Springfield, Missouri . . ."
- If you cannot identify the source of the supporting material you have found on the Internet, do not use it in a scholarly paper or speech. You have no way of assessing the quality of the supporting material absent this information. Try to verify the supporting material you have found from another source, either on the Internet or preferably in print, and use that source instead. If you cannot identify the source of your supporting material, it is the equivalent of using an anonymous source, which is considered inappropriate for scholarly writing and speaking.
- Many Internet sources are dubious in terms of quality. Before using any material obtained from the Internet, especially "free" services such as Google or Yahoo, you should independently confirm the material to ensure accuracy, preferably from a printed source available in your library.
- Different types of support material accomplish different functions in a manuscript or speech. In most cases, it is necessary to use a variety of types of support material so that all of these functions are fulfilled. Avoid the temptation to rely too heavily on supporting material obtained from the Internet because it is convenient to do so. The essence of good speaking and writing is variation in source material. Just as you should not rely solely on supporting material found in newspapers, so too should you not use material found only on the Internet.
- Support material should be balanced in a speech, essay, or research paper. For instance, each main point in a speech must include enough supporting material to adequately support the specific issues being addressed in the point.
- Internet sources of supporting material that have printed equivalents are no better or worse than their printed equivalent. For example, the *New York Times* on the Web is no more or less credible than the *New York Times* in print. The National Rifle Association's printed newsletter is no better or worse then the electronic version of the NRA's newsletter. A source that is incompetent remains incompetent whether in print or on the Internet. One caveat to this statement is that page numbering could be different for online sources, which has implications for how the source should be cited in a bibliography. Generally speaking, documents in PDF format are

electronic replicas of a print version and, consequently, page numbering is the same in both versions. When using a PDF, it is likely that you can cite the source as if it were the print version. When using HTML or other non-PDF versions of documents, it is likely that there is little if any correspondence between page numbers for the electronic version and the print version. In those situations you should cite the source as an electronic document. Thus, while the content might be equivalent, other aspects of the document may or may not be equivalent depending on the file type being used. A reference librarian or your teacher should be able to help you determine exactly what type of file you are using and how you should correctly cite the document in your paper or speech.

We always recommend to our students to print a hard copy of any supporting material they have found on the Internet that they intend to use in a manuscript or speech. That way you have a record of where you found the supporting material that can be provided to your instructor upon request.

CHAPTER THREE
SPECIALIZED WRITING ASSIGNMENTS

In academic writing, some assignments require that you follow standard guidelines for particular types of writing. Among these are speech outlines, annotated bibliographies, research abstracts, research critiques, reviews of literature, and research reports.

COMPOSING A SPEECH OUTLINE

A speech outline is a detailed blueprint for any type of oral presentation. Speech outlines are used for any extemporaneous speaking situations including informative, persuasive, and entertainment speeches. Although the formats for speech outlines vary greatly, most teachers require students to prepare a full-content or preparation outline as well as a speaking outline. Full-content outlines are written in complete sentence format and help the speaker plan the content of the presentation. Full-content outlines include a reference page that should conform to either APA or MLA style. Although APA style guidelines traditionally require a title page, most teachers do not require a title page for a speech outline; you should check with your teacher to determine his or her preference.

The speaking outline might be a typed or handwritten key-word outline that is used to help the speaker deliver the presentation. Your teacher and/or your textbook may provide specific suggestions for composing a speaking outline.

CITING SOURCES

Your preparation outline should include both internal and bibliographic references for sources used in the presentation. Internal source references are how you plan to orally introduce sources in your presentation. For example, you might refer to an article on communication research in this way: "A 1999 study conducted by a communication professor, Mike Allen from the University of Wisconsin Milwaukee, found that sexually explicit images on television . . ." Notice that the internal source reference for an oral presentation is different from an internal citation in a written paper. In an oral presentation, the emphasis is on the qualifications of the source rather than how the source can be verified (i.e., the year or title of the publication). Other techniques for presenting internal source references include:

- As explained in a February 2005 *New York Times* article written by Sandi Elliott, the number of . . .
- The statistics included in this graph came from a report titled "Technology and Education" found on the Department of Education Web site, accessed on March 15, 2005.

- According to the director of the Career Service Center, Dr. Cliff Schuette, whom I interviewed on January 26th . . .

Your full-content outline should contain a bibliographic reference for each internal reference used just as if it were a research paper. The bibliographic references should be listed alphabetically and should conform to either APA or MLA style.

PREPARING THE OUTLINE

Full-content outlines are typically two to four pages in length depending on the nature of the speaking situation and assignment. Your teacher may have specific requirements on the number and types of sources used in your outline. Also, most instructors require that full-content outlines be written in complete sentence format and typed. You can look at a sample full-content outline in Appendixes E (APA) and G (MLA).

- Your outline should contain four section headings: Introduction, Body, Conclusion, and References (or Works Cited). With the exception of the references/works cited section, which is arranged alphabetically, you should renumber points in each section beginning with Roman numeral I.
- Beginning with Roman numeral I set on the left margin, your Introduction section should list all major elements of the introduction. Typically, the major elements would include the attention getter, rationale, credibility statement, and preview. Specific information included under any of these points may need to be indented and identified with capital letters. Recall that one principle of outlining is that if you subdivide a Roman numeral into an A, you should have a corresponding B.
- The Body section should outline the major points you intend to develop to support the central idea of your speech. The first main point should be identified with a flush-left Roman numeral I. Subpoints for any main points should be indented five spaces (one tab) from the left margin and identified with capital letters. Sub-subpoints should be indented 10 spaces (two tabs) from the left margin and identified with regular numbers. Recall that when you subdivide a point, you must have at least two subpoints.
- Any information from external sources (including library research, Internet research, interviews, etc.) should include an internal source reference with some explanation of qualifications.
- Between the introduction and the body of the speech, between main points, and between the body and conclusion of the speech, you should write transition statements. Place the transitional statements in parentheses.
- The Conclusion section typically contains two elements: a summary (designated by Roman numeral I) and a closure statement/call to action (designated by Roman numeral II).

- The Works Cited (MLA) or Reference (APA) section should not use Roman numerals or any other outlining designations, but should list the references in alphabetical order following APA or MLA style.

COMPOSING AN ANNOTATED BIBLIOGRAPHY

An annotated bibliography is a list of sources of information on a specific topic that includes a short summary of the content of each of the works listed. Your instructor may establish specific criteria for topics and work selections. Annotated bibliographies can be written using either the MLA or APA condensed style guides. Each entry in an annotated bibliography provides the reader with two essential pieces of information about the work cited: how to locate the work (source citation) and a brief summary of the contents of the book, book chapter, or journal article (abstract).

CITING SOURCES

In composing an annotated bibliography, follow the rules for citing sources of information in a works cited page (MLA) or references (APA).

THE ABSTRACT

Abstracts can be either brief or extended. Consult with your instructor for any specific instructions regarding the content of an abstract. An extended abstract provides a comprehensive but brief (100–200 word) summary of the contents of a book or article. A brief abstract capsulizes the source's content in 75–100 words. Brief and extended abstracts should be descriptive of the contents of the work cited and not evaluative. Indent the entire abstract five spaces from the left margin.

SAMPLE BRIEF ABSTRACT ENTRY

Williams, D. (1984). 2001: A Space Odyssey: A warning before its

time. *Critical Studies in Mass Communication, 1,* 311–322.

In this article, Williams demonstrates how Kenneth Burke's

concepts of hierarchy and the redemptive process can be used

to analyze and interpret a film rhetorically. Williams suggests that

2001: A Space Odyssey was a warning to the human species to avoid becoming overly dependent on technology and that the ending of the

film offered a religious vision to transcend this technological

dependence.

An extended abstract for a book or theoretical article should contain the following information:

1. a concise statement of the topic;
2. a description of the purpose, thesis, or central construct that guides the work;
3. the sources of information used in the book or article; and
4. the conclusions and implications of the book or article as suggested by the author(s).

An extended abstract for an empirical study should contain the following information:

1. a description of the purpose of the study; the research question(s) or hypothesis(es) studied;
2. a description of the subjects employed in the study including: number, type, age, sex, and selection procedures;
3. a description of how data were collected and analyzed;
4. the results of the study including significance levels where appropriate; and
5. the conclusions and implications of the research as suggested by the authors. (See Appendix B for samples of brief abstracts.)

COMPOSING A RESEARCH CRITIQUE

A critique of a research article contains all the elements of an extended abstract plus a detailed criticism or evaluation of the work cited. Instructors often limit the works you may select to reports of original empirical or humanistic research in the field of Speech Communication. You may also be required to submit a photocopy of the article you have selected along with your critique. A research critique can be written using either the MLA or APA condensed style guides. See Chapter 1 for a representative list of scholarly journals that may contain reports of original empirical or humanistic research. A sample research critique is provided in Appendix C.

CITING SOURCES

In composing a research critique, follow the rules for citing sources of information in a works cited (MLA) or references page (APA).

THE CRITIQUE

A critique of a research article provides important information about an empirical or humanistic research article in two parts: (1) a summary of the article (abstract) and (2) a critique of the article. A typical research critique will average between 1,000 and 1,500 words in length. In the summary (abstract) of an original empirical or humanistic study, include the following information:

1. a brief statement of the purpose and rationale of the study;
2. the research question(s) or hypothesis(es) studied;
3. a description of the subjects employed in the study including: number, type, age, sex, and selection procedures;
4. a description of the method(s) employed, including the content of surveys, questionnaires, or interviews and the procedures used to collect and analyze the data;
5. the results of the study, including significance levels where appropriate; and
6. the conclusions and implications of the research as suggested by the authors.

Your instructor may provide you with specific criteria to use in evaluating original empirical or humanistic studies. An excellent resource for reading and evaluating communication research is *Interpreting Communication Research: A Case Study Approach* by L. R. Frey, C. H. Botan, P. G. Friedman, and G. L. Kreps (1992, Prentice Hall). Absent specific instructions, apply the following criteria in critiquing original research:

1. **Theoretical scope:** Does the study apply to a broad domain of the communication process? How might we extend the knowledge provided by the study to other contexts?
2. **Appropriateness of methodology:** Are the study's methodology and reporting of results appropriate for answering the proposed research question(s) and/or hypothesis(es)?
3. **Validity:** Does the study satisfy the requirements for external and internal validity?
4. **External validity** is the extent to which the results of the study can be generalized beyond the conditions created by the researchers. **Internal validity** questions whether the study was internally consistent and whether or not it addressed what it claimed to address.
5. **Heuristic value:** Do the study's methodology, results, and conclusions help to generate future research? Are the conclusions nonobvious?
6. **Parsimony:** Relative to other studies, does this study provide the simplest, most logical explanation of the area being studied? Was the design of the study only as complicated as it needed to be to test the hypothesis(es) or research question(s)?

COMPOSING A REVIEW OF LITERATURE

A review of literature is a summary of previous research relative to a given topic or question. A review of literature should give the reader a clear overview of what is known about the topic, including summaries of research conclusions, various methods used to investigate the topic, and indications of what areas remain to be investigated. A review of literature differs from an annotated bibliography by providing more than separate summaries of the sources included. Reviews of literature point out common themes in existing research and draw conclusions about the "state of the art" regarding knowledge in the given area. Researchers generally conduct and write a review of literature prior to proposing a specific research project in order to determine what important questions remain to be explored and to provide a rationale for their specific study.

A review of literature is a common writing assignment, one that may serve as the culmination of a course or the first step in a larger research project like a thesis or dissertation. Your instructor may give you specific instructions regarding the length of your review of literature and the scope of sources that must be included. A review of literature might range from a paper of a few pages to a dissertation chapter of more than 100 pages. In composing a review of literature, follow the guidelines of either the MLA or APA condensed style guides, including a works cited (MLA) or references (APA) page. See Appendix D for a study that includes a review of literature.

Here is a common format for a review of literature:

1. **Introduction:** Introduce the topic and provide a preview of what is to follow in the paper.
2. **Problem statement** (also known as Rationale): Briefly describe the significance of the research you are reviewing and/or the importance of conducting such a review. There are two basic strategies for articulating rationale. One strategy is called **negative rationale,** where you might argue that previous research has failed to address a particular area of concern. Another strategy is called **positive rationale,** where you might claim there would be practical or theoretical benefits to exploring some topic in more detail. Positive rationale is generally perceived as the strongest of the two strategies.
3. **Review:** The review is more than just a string of individual abstracts. It is a thorough review organized around a specific thesis. The problem statement should provide clear focus for the review. Clear and smooth transitions between main points are especially important. The reader should be guided to a clear conclusion by the information and arguments presented in the review. In a review of literature, some sources may be treated in great detail, while others are mentioned only briefly as examples or supporting evidence.

A common mistake made by less experienced writers is that their literature reviews read like a list of article summaries with little or no connective analysis. Think of the body of your literature review as the body of a speech. Most of what is written should be your ideas and analysis. In essence, you should make carefully supported arguments about how readers should interpret previous literature, how they should understand theory, or how they should observe conceptual gaps. Your analysis is essential for establishing a compelling rationale for your study and provides the logical flow of ideas that tie elements of the literature review together. Source citations might be liberally used to support claims that you make; however, direct quotations are typically used only when the exact wording found in another source is essential to your own argument.

4. **Conclusion:** Restate the thesis of your paper and summarize key points. Indicate the implications of the review, such as any new research questions, applications of existing research, or integration of diverse sources.

In his book *Research Design: Qualitative, Quantitative, and Mixed Method Approaches,* John Cresswell (2002) recommends designing a map, or visual rendering, of the research literature. As part of the map, the writer builds a visual representation of major topics discussed in the literature as well as potential avenues for further exploration.

To illustrate how a visual map of literature facilitates writing a review, read the sample research report in Appendix D. The literature review for that report can be mapped using an inverted funnel as a visual representation. Notice how the review begins by discussing the general concept of note taking effectiveness. Next, the review explains general strategies teachers can use to improve student note taking. Finally, the literature review discusses a specific strategy, called organizational lecture cues, in terms of how that strategy could improve students' note taking. An inverted funnel is an appropriate visual representation for this literature review because it begins with general information found in literature and then presents progressively more-specific information. Using such a map, or visual representation, prior to writing the literature review would help the authors of this report determine how to organize the ideas discussed in the review. Although the inverted funnel makes sense for the literature reviewed in this report, other reports might use different visual representations like concept maps or flow charts illustrating connections between specific topics.

COMPOSING A RESEARCH REPORT

A research report provides the reader with specific information about a piece of original, empirical research that the author has conducted. You are in essence reporting the design and results of your research project to a larger community.

A research report follows the same general format found in journal articles reporting original empirical or humanistic research. The length of a research report will vary depending on the complexity of the study, the space devoted to reviewing past research, and the nature of the data being reported. Research reports may be prepared following either the MLA or APA condensed style guides. An example research report is included in Appendix D. Your instructor may give you specific guidelines to follow, but most research reports follow a standard format that includes the following:

1. **A statement of the purpose of the research,** often stated in terms of a "research problem" that needs to be addressed (see previous section on composing a literature review for information on articulating problem statements and reviewing literature);

2. **A review of past research** (review of literature) relevant to the research topic, demonstrating the author's understanding of the area and building a rationale for the present study. It should be clear to the reader how your study is positioned within the concepts and theories discussed in existing literature;

3. **A statement of the study's hypothesis(es)** and/or research question(s), justified on the basis of the review of literature;

4. **A description of the methods employed in the study,** which for empirical studies includes the study's participants, data-gathering methods/procedures, evidence of the reliability and validity of measures, and data-analysis procedures; for humanistic studies, it includes the criteria used in selecting texts or events for analysis and the theoretical or methodological approach taken to analyze data;

5. **A summary of the study's results,** including specific answers for each of the research question(s) and/or hypothesis(es); and

6. **A discussion of the implications of the results,** explanations for the results, limitations of the research, and suggestions for future research in the topic area.

CHAPTER FOUR
A CONDENSED MLA STYLE GUIDE

FORMATTING THE TEXT OF YOUR PAPER

TYPING

Unless you are otherwise instructed, type all written work submitted for evaluation. The type must be clear, dark, and easily readable. Laser-quality output has become the minimum acceptable standard for instructors as well as prospective employers. Use only standard typefaces such as Courier or Prestige Elite (standard typewriter faces), Helvetica or Times Roman (standard word-processing type faces) or their equivalents, and standard type sizes (10 or 12 point). Only type on one side of the paper. Never use "fancy" or unusual fonts. Do not use full justification; keep the right-hand margin ragged.

PAPER

Use only heavy (20 pound or heavier) white, 8.5 by 11-inch bond paper. Never submit any work typed on erasable or "onion skin" paper. If you use erasable paper, have a high-quality photocopy made on heavy white, 8.5 by 11-inch bond paper and submit the photocopy to your instructor. Keep the original copy for your files.

MARGINS

Leave one-inch margins at the top, bottom, left, and right of your paper. Nothing should appear within this one-inch margin except pagination. Indent the first word of each paragraph five spaces from the left margin and set off quotations 10 spaces from the left margin. Do not indent the first word of a set-off quotation. A set-off quotation is any quotation of more than four typed lines. Do not justify the right margin.

LINE SPACING

Your paper should be double-spaced throughout, including the heading, title, text, quotations, and works cited.

TITLE PAGE

MLA does not require a formal, separate title page. Instead, type your name, your instructor's name, the course name and number, and the date at the top of the first page flush with the left margin. Note that MLA follows the (day, month, year) format. Type and center the title of the paper two spaces below the heading. Double-space between the title and the first line of the text of the paper. If your instructor specifically requires that you have a formal, separate title page for your paper, follow the model on the following page. If you are required to provide a formal title page, do not repeat the author, instructor, course, and date information that appears on the formal title page on the first page of the text of the paper. Repeat the title of the paper and double-space to the first line of text.

MLA RULE BOX 1

Wagon 1

Chuck Wagon
[2 spaces]
Ms. Deborah Craig
[2 spaces]
COM 205 Interpersonal Communication
[2 spaces]
12 September 2008
[2 spaces]

Self-Disclosure Among Dual Career Couples
[2 spaces from title to first line of text]

Increasingly, dual career couples have become the norm in our

society rather than the exception. Unfortunately, relatively little is known

about the communication patterns among dual-career couples.

MLA RULE BOX 2

[start pagination ½ inch from top and right]
Wagon 2
[space ½ inch to the first line of text on the page]

First line of the text on the page appears ½ inch below the pagination

for the page for a total top margin of 1 inch.

Self-Disclosure Among Dual Career Couples

Chuck Wagon

Organizational Communication 336

Dr. Lynn Harter

12 September 2008

PAGINATION

All scholarly writing requires pagination. Number each of the pages consecutively throughout the manuscript. Place all pagination in the upper right-hand corner, ½ inch from the top and ½ inch from the right of the page. Include your last name preceding each page number. Do not punctuate the page number in any way. The first page of the manuscript is the page on which the text of the manuscript begins. In MLA, a formal title page is not counted as a page of the manuscript.

CITING SOURCES IN THE TEXT OF YOUR PAPER

MLA style uses parenthetical references for citing sources. Parenthetical references are placed within the text of the paper rather than at the bottom of each page (footnotes) or at the end of the paper (endnotes). The basic format for an MLA parenthetical reference is: (author's last name, followed by a space and the page(s) upon which the cited information can be found). For example:

> Native English speakers tend to receive significantly higher scores
>
> on The Speaking Proficiency English Assessment Kit (SPEAK) than
>
> non-native English speakers (Powell 40).

As a way of adding variety to your citations, mention the author's name in the text and cite the page number parenthetically. For example:

> Powell demonstrated that native English speakers tend to receive
>
> significantly higher scores on The Speaking Proficiency English
>
> Assessment Kit (SPEAK) than non-native English speakers (40).

When citing an entire work, the most elegant citation is to include the author (and possibly the work) in the text and omit the parenthetical reference entirely.

> In <u>Thriving on Chaos: Handbook for a Management Revolution,</u>
>
> Tom Peters shatters many of the conventional myths regarding
>
> effective management.

or

> Peters shatters many of the conventional myths regarding effective
>
> management in his book, <u>Thriving on Chaos: Handbook for a</u>
>
> <u>Management Revolution.</u>

Follow the same rules for citing a direct quotation.

> "In general, the present findings suggest that little has changed over
>
> the past thirty years in the textbook treatment of communication
>
> apprehension" (Pelias 51).

A direct quotation or close paraphrase requires a page citation in the parenthetical reference. There are no exceptions to this rule.

The same rules apply when citing a source with two or three authors.

> "It is our belief and the belief of prospective employers throughout
>
> the United States that courses such as public speaking, listening, and
>
> interpersonal communication should be included as an oral
>
> communication core in such a blended program" (Curtis, Winsor,
>
> and Stephens 13).

When citing a work with more than three authors, name the first author and include the abbreviation "et al." (meaning "and others") followed by a space and page number(s).

> "Authority, personal experience, intuition, custom, and magic may
>
> be good starting points for the systematic pursuit of knowledge, but
>
> they don't necessarily lead to valid knowledge about the world"
>
> (Frey et al. 6).

When a direct quotation exceeds four typed lines in length, MLA requires that the quotation be set off from the rest of the text. Introduce and cite the quotation as you would normally, omit the quotation marks, indent the entire quotation 10 spaces from the left margin, and type it in block form within the text. For example:

> This particular study raises a number of issues that have heuristic
>
> value.
>
> > The anxiety actually experienced during the communication
> >
> > event was not thought to affect the CA trait. In fact, reducing CA

was discussed in terms of clinical treatment such as systematic

desensitization. The results of the present study indicate that

communication state anxiety experiences could reduce trait CA.

(McCroskey et al. 181-2)

MLA RULE BOX 3

In MLA, the correct punctuation for a block quotation goes at the end of the last word of the quotation, not at the end of the citation. Do not include any punctuation at the end of the citation.

When citing a single work by an author of two or more works in the text of your paper, include the author's last name followed by a comma and the complete title (if relatively short) or an abbreviated version of the full title (if relatively long).

All groups develop fluid status hierarchies over time (Bourhis,

"Status in Small Groups"). The gradual development of these status

hierarchies has a profound effect upon role development (Bourhis,

"Role Development in Small Groups") as well as the formation of

normative behavior (Bourhis, "Norms").

CITING SOURCES OBTAINED ELECTRONICALLY

The goal of any form of citation is to allow you or someone else interested in your topic to retrieve the information you have used in your manuscript. Your citation must be complete and must allow someone else to retrace your steps in obtaining the information electronically. With electronic citations, it is especially important that punctuation and capitalization be accurate in the address. Use standard MLA rules and conventions for citing authors and sources discussed previously in this section, including rules for capitalization. The MLA home page provides the following guidelines for citing electronic material:

- Identify the name of the author, editor, compiler, or translator of the source (if available), reversed for alphabetizing and followed by any appropriate abbreviations (e.g., Ed.).

- Identify the title of the work whether it be a speech, poem, or article. If it is a posting from a discussion list, provide the title from the subject line in quotation marks followed by the descriptor online posting. If the source is a Web page, underline the title of the page or indicate some descriptor like home page if no title is provided.
- Provide the date of publication or of the last update if available. For discussion group postings or electronic mail, indicate the date of the message.
- Name the institution, sponsoring organization, or discussion group responsible for producing the source.
- Indicate the date that the material was accessed by the researcher.
- Provide a complete electronic address or URL of the source in angle brackets.

MLA RULE BOX 4

When must I document a source?

You must document a source whenever you:
1. Directly quote, word-for-word, someone else's work;
2. Paraphrase or summarize someone else's work; and
3. Use facts and data that are not common knowledge.

As a general rule, when in doubt, provide a citation. You will rarely be penalized by your instructor for giving credit to someone's work.

In general, these guidelines require electronic sources to follow the following format that can readily be adapted to various forms of electronic material:

Author's last name, first name. "Title of Specific Article, Web File, or

Online Posting." <u>Underline the Web Site Title</u> or use a descriptor like

Online Posting. Date of Publication or Revision. Name of Sponsoring

Institution. Date Accessed <Complete Electronic Address>.

PRIMARY VERSUS SECONDARY SOURCE MATERIAL

To properly evaluate sources, you need to determine whether or not your supporting material is from a primary or secondary source. Primary source material (direct) is the raw data, information, or opinion of an author. Secondary source material (indirect) is raw data, information, or opinion that has been summarized by someone other than the original creator. If someone conducts a study that examines the relationship between communication apprehension and academic achievement and publishes the results of the study, that author is a primary source. If another author quotes the original article and you read that quotation, you are reading a secondary source. For example, when citing a textbook you are often relying on a secondary source—the author of the textbook who is summarizing work done by others. You are trusting that the author of the text has read and analyzed primary source material and is accurately and objectively summarizing that material in the text.

MLA RULE BOX 5

As a general rule, it is always preferable to rely on primary versus secondary source material in your writing. Reliance on primary source material results in scholarship that is more credible and persuasive. For this reason, graduate students may be required to use only primary source material in their scholarly writing, particularly for their thesis and dissertation.

CITING A SECONDARY SOURCE IN YOUR MANUSCRIPT

To document to the reader that you are relying upon secondary source material in your manuscript, use the abbreviation "qtd. in" ("quoted in") in your text citation. In the list of works cited, only include the source you consulted (secondary source), not the primary source you are citing.

> Celia Green once wrote that, "The way to do research is to attack the
>
> facts at the point of greatest astonishment" (qtd. in Reinhard 183).

In this example, Celia Green is the primary source and John Reinhard is the secondary source. In the list of works cited, the citation would read:

Jane 12

Works Cited

Reinhard, John. Introduction to Communication Research. 3rd ed.

   Boston: McGraw-Hill, 2000.

SAMPLE MLA ENTRIES

BOOKS

The basic format for a book entry includes: author's name; title of part of book; title of the book; editor, translator, or compiler; edition; place of publication; publisher; and date of publication.

1. BOOK WITH ONE AUTHOR

Fairhurst, Gail. <u>Discursive Leadership: In Conversation with Leadership Psychology</u>. Thousand Oaks, CA: Sage Publications, 2007.

2. BOOK WITH TWO AUTHORS

Galanes, Gloria, and Katherine Adams. <u>Effective Group Decisions: Theory and Practice</u>. 12th ed. Boston: McGraw-Hill, 2007.

MLA RULE BOX 6

How do I know which words to capitalize in the title of a book?

In book titles and subtitles, capitalize the first word, the last word, and all principal words. Capitalize all nouns, pronouns, adjectives, and adverbs. Do not capitalize coordinating conjunctions (e.g., and, but, for, nor, or) or prepositions introducing phrases (e.g., of, before, in, to). Do not capitalize an article (e.g., a, an, the) unless it is the first word in a title. Separate titles from subtitles with a colon and capitalize the first word after the colon. Include any other punctuation that is part of the title.

---

3. BOOK WITH THREE OR MORE AUTHORS

Nelson, Paul, et al. <u>Public Speaking: A Guide for the Engaged Communicator</u>. Boston: McGraw-Hill, 2007.

4. TWO OR MORE BOOKS BY THE SAME AUTHOR

Orbe, Mark. <u>Constructing Co-Cultural Theory: An Explication of Culture, Power, and Communication</u>. Thousand Oaks, CA: Sage Publications, 1998.

---. <u>Interracial Communication</u>. 2nd ed. Thousand Oaks, CA: Sage Publications, 2007.

5. BOOK WITH AN EDITOR

May, Steve, ed. <u>Case Studies in Organizational Communication: Ethical Perspectives and Practices</u>. Thousand Oaks, CA: Sage Publications, 2006.

---

6. BOOK WITH TWO EDITORS

Craig, Robert, and Heidi Muller, eds. Theorizing Communication: Readings

Across Traditions. Thousand Oaks, CA: Sage Publications, 2007.

7. AN EDITION OTHER THAN THE FIRST

West, Richard, and Lynn Turner. Introducing Communication Theory: Analysis

and Application. 3rd ed. Boston: McGraw-Hill, 2007.

8. A WORK IN A BOOK

Miller, Katherine. "Communication as Constructive." Communication As:

Perspectives on Theory. Eds. Gregory Shephard, Jeffrey John, and Ted

Striphas. Thousand Oaks, CA: Sage Publications, 2006. 31-37.

MLA RULE BOX 7

The page numbers at the end of the citation indicate the first and last pages of the work in a book. Type two-digit page numbers as they appear in the book. If the first digit of three-digit page numbers is identical, delete the first digit of the second page number (e.g., 201-02).

---

9. A TRANSLATION

Aristotle. The Rhetoric. Trans. W. Rys Roberts. New York: Modern Library,

1954.

Cicero. Rhetorica ad Herennium. Trans. Harry Caplan. Cambridge: Harvard

University Press, 1954.

ARTICLES

The basic format for an article entry includes: author's name; title of article; name of periodical (underlined) and volume number; date of publication; and page numbers. The page numbers at the end of the citation indicate the first and last pages of the article. Type two-digit page numbers as they appear in the article. If the first two digits of three-digit page numbers are identical, delete the first digit of the second page number (201-02). If the first two digits of four-digit page numbers are identical, delete the first two digits of the second page number (1112-13).

10. ARTICLE WITH ONE AUTHOR

Abelman, Robert. "Fighting the War on Indecency: Mediating TV, Internet, and

    Videogame Usage Among Achieving and Underachieving Gifted Children."

    Roeper Review 29 (2007): 100-12.

Aubrey, Jennifer. "The Impact of Sexually Objectifying Media Exposure on

    Negative Body Emotions and Sexual Self-Perceptions: Investigating the

    Mediating Role of Body Self-Consciousness." Mass Communication &

    Society 10 (2007): 1-23.

MLA RULE BOX 8

How do I know which words to capitalize in article and journal titles?

Follow the rules for capitalizing words in book titles.

---

11. ARTICLE WITH TWO OR THREE AUTHORS

Barge, Kevin, and David Schlueter. "Memorable Messages and Newcomer

    Socialization." Western Journal of Communication 68 (2004): 233-57.

Mazer, Joseph, Richard Murphy, and Cheri Simonds. "I'll See You on

    'Facebook': The Effects of Computer-Mediated Teacher Self-Disclosure on

    Student Motivation, Affective Learning, and Classroom Climate."

    Communication Education 56 (2007): 1-17.

12. ARTICLE WITH FOUR OR MORE AUTHORS

English, Eric, Steven Llano, Gordon Mitchell, Catherine Morrison, John Rief,

    and Carly Woods. "Debate as a Weapon of Mass Destruction."

    Communication & Critical/Cultural Studies 4 (2007): 221-25.

13. ARTICLE IN A MONTHLY OR BIMONTHLY PERIODICAL

For a periodical entry, do not put the date in parentheses.

Flynn, Stephen. "The Neglected Home Front." <u>Foreign Affairs</u>. Sept.–Oct. 2004:

20-33.

Weiner, Lauren. "Islam and Women." <u>Policy Review</u>. Oct.–Nov. 2004: 49-66.

14. ARTICLE IN A WEEKLY OR BIWEEKLY PERIODICAL

Cowley, Geoffrey. "The Flu Shot Fiasco." <u>Newsweek</u>. 1 November 2004: 40-44.

Gibbs, Nancy. "The Morning After." <u>Time</u>. 1 November 2004: 28-34.

NEWSPAPERS

The basic format for a newspaper entry includes: author's name; article title (in quotation marks); name of newspaper (underlined); type of edition (if available); date; and page. Newspaper articles are not always paginated continuously. An article might start on the front page and skip to page 10. If the article is not continuously paginated, indicate the first page of the article followed by a plus sign.

15. SIGNED ARTICLE FROM A DAILY NEWSPAPER

Regan, Tom. "Maybe E-mail Isn't Such a Great Idea, After All." <u>Christian Science</u>

<u>Monitor</u> 17 Oct. 2007: 16.

MLA RULE BOX 9

When citing an article in a journal or periodical, when do I use quotation marks and when do I underline?

Place the full title of an article in quotation marks. Put the appropriate concluding punctuation before the closing quotation mark. Underline the name of the periodical or journal.

---

16. UNSIGNED ARTICLE FROM A DAILY NEWSPAPER

"Your Career." <u>The Boston Globe</u> 14 Oct. 2007: V8.

17. SIGNED EDITORIAL FROM A DAILY NEWSPAPER

The basic format for a newspaper editorial includes: author's name; article title (in quotation marks); the description "Editorial"; name of newspaper (underlined); type of edition (if available); date; and page.

Young, Cathy. "Radicalism in the Deaf Culture." Editorial. The Boston Globe

6 Nov. 2006: A13.

18. UNSIGNED EDITORIAL FROM A DAILY NEWSPAPER

"On the Heights of Excellence: Best School Systems Around the World Avoid

Distractions Such as Faith-Based Funding." Editorial. The Toronto Star

30 Sept. 2007: A25.

MANUSCRIPTS

19. UNPUBLISHED MANUSCRIPT

Striley, Catherine. "The Multiple Realities of Gifted Children: Socially

Constructing the Duality of Privilege and Marginalization." Unpublished

manuscript. 2007.

20. UNPUBLISHED PAPER PRESENTED AT PROFESSIONAL MEETING

Bohlman, Daniel, and Lindsey Harness. "Sunday Morning Drivers: A Content

Analysis of Topic Choice and Frequency in Sunday Morning News Shows."

National Communication Association, Nov. 2007, Chicago.

21. PERSONAL INTERVIEWS

The basic format for citing an interview that you have personally conducted includes: the name of the person interviewed; the kind of interview you conducted (e.g., telephone, e-mail interview, personal interview); and the date.

Striley, Catherine. Telephone interview. 28 Sept. 2007.

Tenzek, Kelly. Personal interview. 15 Oct. 2007.

PUBLIC LECTURES

The basic format for a lecture includes: lecturer's name; title of the lecture (in quotation marks); the sponsoring organization, meeting, or group; place where the lecture was delivered; and date. If there is no title, use an appropriate descriptive label (e.g., lecture, address, presentation, speech, discussion).

22. CLASS LECTURE

Bauman, Isabelle. "Structuration Theory." Missouri State University,

Springfield. 25 Oct. 2007.

23. TWO OR MORE LECTURES BY THE SAME SPEAKER

Morris, Taleyna. "Uncertainty Reduction Theory." Missouri State University,

Springfield. 7 Feb. 2007.

---. "Expectancy Violations Theory." Missouri State University, Springfield.

22 Feb. 2007.

---. "Elaboration Likelihood Model." Missouri State University, Springfield.

28 Feb. 2007.

24. FILMS

The basic format for a film includes: title of film; director; distributor; and year. You may include other data that are pertinent (e.g., performers).

The Four Seasons. Dir. Alan Alda. Perf. Alan Alda, Carol Burnett, Len Cariou,

Sandy Dennis, Rita Moreno, Jack Weston, and Bess Armstrong.

Universal, 1981.

The Breakfast Club. Dir. John Hughes. Perf. Emilio Estevez, Judd Nelson,

Molly Ringwald, Anthony Hall, and Ally Sheedy. Universal, 1985.

25. TELEVISION PROGRAMS

The basic format for citing a television program includes: title of the episode, segment, or story (in quotation marks); title of the program (underlined like a book title); title of the series; name of the network (e.g., ABC, CBS, NBC, FOX); call letters and city of the local station (if available); and date the program was broadcast. If you are citing a transcript of a television program, add "Transcription" at the end of the citation.

"Who Killed Stephanie Crowe?" Narr. Bill Lagatutta. <u>48 Hours</u>. CBS. WCBS,

New York. 9 Oct. 2004.

"John Carey on Clinton's Support." Narr. Chris Matthews. <u>Hardball</u>. MSNBC,

25 Oct. 2004. Transcription.

26. RADIO BROADCASTS

The basic format for citing a radio program includes: title of the episode, segment, or story (in quotation marks); title of the program (underlined like a book title); title of the series; name of the network (e.g., Air America, NPR, CNN, Turner Broadcasting); call letters and city of the local station (if available); and date the program was broadcast. If you are citing a transcript of a radio program, add "Transcription" at the end of the citation.

"Late Singer Merrill Expanded Opera's Audience." Narr. Jeffrey Freymann.

<u>Arts and Culture</u>. Natl. Public Radio. 26 Oct. 2004. Transcription.

27. ENCYCLOPEDIA OR DICTIONARY

The basic format for citing an article/definition in an encyclopedia or dictionary includes: article title or word; title of the encyclopedia or dictionary (underlined); edition; and year.

"The Internet." <u>Cambridge Advanced Learner's Dictionary</u>. 2003.

"Quintilian." <u>Columbia Encyclopedia</u>. 6th ed. 2004.

ELECTRONIC SOURCES

28. INTERNET SOURCES

The citation for an Internet source should include enough information that someone else could find the same source using the citation provided. Think of your citation as a map to finding the source you are using. The basic format for an Internet source includes: author's name; title of the document (in quotation marks); any information about a printed equivalent; date of original publication; date you accessed the source; and the URL. In those cases where information is not provided, cite as much as is available.

Foster, Andrea. "Video Games with a Political Message." The Chronicle of

Higher Education. 29 Oct. 2004. 1 Sept. 2007 <http://chronicle.com/prm/

weekly/v51/i10/10a03201.htm>.

29. ELECTRONIC COLLECTION

"AECT Publications." Association for Educational Communications and

Technology Home Page. 27 April 1998. Association for Educational

Communications and Technology. 5 May 2007 <http://204.252.76.75:80/

Pubs/aectpubs.html>.

Oetting, Dan. "Eugene Debs: The Issue." Douglass: Archives of American

Public Address. 14 April 1998. Northwestern University. 5 May 2007

<http://douglass.speech.nwu.edu/debs_a80.htm>.

Trent, Judith. "An Invitation to Play a Role in NCA's Governance." National

Communication Association Home Page. 1998. National Communication

Association. 5 May 2007 <http://www.natcom.org/aboutNCA/leadership/

Invitation.html>.

30. DISCUSSION LIST

Driver, Dutch. "Applying Communication to COMGRADS." Online posting.

12 May 2007. COMGRADS Hotline <COMGRADS@CIOS.org>.

Moreale, Sherry. "NCA Poster Session Task Force Report." Online posting.

11 May 2007. CRTNET News <crtnet@natcom.org>.

31. ELECTRONIC MAIL (E-MAIL)

To cite electronic mail, provide the name of the author of the e-mail; the title of the e-mail (enclosed in quotation marks if available); a brief description of the e-mail message; and the date of the message.

Dorrough, Angie. "Response to Dr. Bourhis' Request for Information." E-mail to

Dr. John Bourhis. 6 August 2007.

Johnston, Chad. "Requirements for Speech Three Assignment." E-mail to the

author. 27 June 2007.

32. ARTICLE IN AN ONLINE PUBLICATION

The basic format for citing an online article includes all of the information for citing a printed article plus the date of access and the URL.

Dargis, Manohla. "Human Frailty and Pain on Boston's Mean Streets." New York

Times on the Web. 19 Oct. 2007. 30 Oct. 2007 <http://movies.nytimes.com/

2007/10/19/movies/19gone.html?8mu&emc=mua1>.

Labaton, Stephen. "Media Companies Succeed in Easing Ownership Limits." New

York Times on the Web. 16 April 2007. 1 May 2007 <http://www.nytimes.com/

2001/04/16/business/16MEDI.html>.

33. ONLINE BOOK

The basic format for an online book includes all of the information required for a printed book plus the date of access and the URL.

Kelly, Kevin. Out of Control. 1994. 2 May 2007 <http://www.well.com/user/kk/

OutOfControl/>.

34. HOME PAGE IN SUPPORT OF A COURSE

To cite a home page in support of a course, give the name of the instructor; title of the course; a brief description of the page; the beginning and ending dates of the course; the academic department in which the course is offered; the name of the institution; the date the Internet page was accessed; and the URL.

Bourhis, John. Communication, Community and Conflict. Course home page for

COM 511. Aug. 2005–Dec. 2005. Department of Communication, Missouri

State University. 4 Nov. 2007 <http://eschool.missouristate.edu/bin/

common/course.pl.>.

35. HOME PAGE IN SUPPORT OF AN ACADEMIC DEPARTMENT

To cite a home page in support of an academic department, give the name of the academic department; a brief description of the page; the name of the academic institution at which the department resides; the date the Internet page was accessed; and the URL.

Communication. Departmental home page. Missouri State University. 6 June

2007 <http://communication.missouristate.edu/>.

PREPARING THE LIST OF WORKS CITED

The list of works cited appears at the end of the paper. Begin the list on a new page and number each page. Continue with the page numbers of the text. The title "Works Cited" appears centered at the top of the page. Double-space between the title and the first entry. Begin each entry flush with the left margin. If the entry runs more than one line in length, indent the second and each subsequent line of the entry five spaces from the left margin. Double-space the entire list, both between and within entries.

Arrange the entries in the list of works cited in alphabetical order by the author's last name. If the author's name is unknown, alphabetize the entry by the first word of the title other than "A," "An," and "The." For example: "The Recession Is Coming" would be alphabetized under "R" in the list of works cited.

In citing two or more works by the same author in the works cited list, cite the author's name in the first entry only. Thereafter, use three hyphens (---) followed by a period, skip two spaces, and give the title.

MLA RULE BOX 10

Jones 8

Works Cited

McNeil, Stacy. "Classical Theory." Missouri State University, Springfield.

15 Sept. 2007.

---. "Systems Theory." Missouri State University, Springfield. 23 Oct.

2007.

Wilmot, William, and Joyce Hocker. Interpersonal Conflict. 7th ed.

New York: McGraw-Hill.

CHAPTER FIVE
A CONDENSED APA STYLE GUIDE

FORMATTING THE TEXT OF YOUR PAPER

TYPING

Unless otherwise instructed, all written work submitted for evaluation must be typed. The type must be clear, dark, and easily readable. Laser-quality output has become the minimum acceptable standard for instructors as well as prospective employers. Use only standard typefaces such as Courier or Prestige Elite (standard typewriter faces), Helvetica or Times Roman (standard word-processing type faces) or their equivalents, and standard type sizes (10 or 12 point). Only type on one side of the paper. Never use "fancy" or unusual fonts. Do not justify the right margin.

PAPER

Use only heavy, white, 8.5 by 11-inch bond paper. Never submit any work typed on erasable or "onion skin" paper. If you use erasable paper, have a high-quality photocopy made on heavy, white, 8.5 by 11-inch bond paper and submit the photocopy to your instructor. Keep the original copy for your files.

INDEX TO APA RULE BOXES

MARGINS

The newest edition of APA allows you to set your margins at either 1 inch or 1.5 inches top, bottom, left, and right. Consult your instructor to see if she has a particular preference. Whichever size margins you choose, be consistent throughout the entire manuscript. Nothing should appear within the margins.

Indent the first word of each paragraph five to seven spaces from the left margin. Quotations in excess of 40 words should be indented five spaces from the left margin, double-spaced, and without the usual paragraph indentation. Quotations in excess of 40 words and more than one paragraph in length should have the second and each additional paragraph indented five spaces from the new margin.

LINE SPACING

Your paper should be double-spaced throughout, including the heading, title, text, quotations, and references page.

Magic Kingdom 1

Running head: MAGIC KINGDOM

Entering and Exiting the Magic Kingdom:

How Metaphors Are Used During the Organizational Assimilation

Process at Disney World

John Doe

Concordia College

TITLE PAGE

APA requires that your paper have a title page. The components of a title page are: the title of your paper, your name, institutional affiliation, and a running head. The title must also appear centered at the top of the first page of your paper followed by two spaces before the text of the paper begins. In APA, the preferred form of an author's name is first name, middle initial, and last name. Institutional affiliation refers to where the author(s) conducted the research. This includes your school. The running head is an abbreviated title that is printed at the top of the pages of a published manuscript to identify the article for readers. On your title page, type the running head in uppercase letters, flush left two lines below the pagination line. Beginning with the title, type the remaining information centered on the page, as shown in the example title page and in the sample papers in the appendixes.

PAGINATION

All scholarly writing requires pagination. Number all of the pages consecutively throughout the manuscript. Page "1" of the manuscript is the title page. Place all pagination in the upper right-hand corner, 1½ inches from the top and 1½ inches from the right of the page—depending on which margin size you have chosen. Remember, keep the margin area clear so your instructor has a place to make comments. To identify the manuscript, type the first two or three words from the title in the upper right-hand corner five spaces to the left of the page number. Do not punctuate the page number in any way.

Magic Kingdom 1

BINDING

Unless otherwise instructed, neatly staple the pages of your paper together in the upper left-hand corner. Do not tape, pin, or tear the corner(s) to bind the pages of your paper together. Unless specifically instructed to do so, do not submit your paper in a binder of any kind. Such bindings often make it difficult for instructors to easily grade your paper.

ABSTRACTS

APA requires an abstract for all papers/articles being submitted to a convention for presentation or to a journal for review and possible publication. Normally, this requirement is waived for the typical undergraduate paper. However, in special cases, your instructor may require that you write an abstract for your paper.

An abstract provides a comprehensive but brief (75–100 words) summary of the contents of a paper/article. The abstract should be descriptive of the contents of the work cited, not evaluative. Do not indent the first word of the abstract.

An abstract for a theoretical article should contain the following information:

1. a concise statement of the topic;
2. a description of the purpose, thesis, or central construct that guides the work;
3. the sources of information used in the book or article; and
4. the conclusions and implications of the book or article as suggested by the author(s).

An abstract for an empirical study should contain the following information:

1. the research question(s) or hypothesis(es) studied;
2. a description of the subjects employed in the study including: number, type, age, sex, and selection procedures;
3. a description of the experimental method(s) employed;
4. the results of the study including significance levels where appropriate; and
5. the conclusions and implications of the research as suggested by the author(s).

Abstract

A meta-analysis of 183 experiments comparing the effect sizes of measurement techniques for assessing the effectiveness of public speaking anxiety treatments was conducted. The comparison showed differences between self-report, observer, and physiological measurement techniques. However, no interaction was observed between the type of therapy and the type of measurement technique. The implications for measuring public speaking anxiety and the classroom application of the results are considered.

CITING SOURCES IN THE TEXT OF YOUR PAPER

APA style uses parenthetical references for citing sources. Parenthetical references are placed within the text of the paper rather than at the bottom of each page (footnotes) or at the end of the paper (endnotes). The basic format for an APA parenthetical reference is: (author's last name, followed by a comma and space, and the year in which the work was published).

For example:

> Surprisingly, television probably is more conservative than other
>
> media in its portrayal of family life (Albada, 2000).

As a way of adding variety to your citations, mention the author's name in the text and include the year parenthetically. For example:

> Albada (2000) suggests that television probably is more
>
> conservative than other media in its portrayal of family life.

When citing an entire work, the most elegant citation is to include the author (and possibly the work) in the text and include the year parenthetically.

> In *The Corporate Culture Survival Guide,* Edgar Schein (1999)
>
> provides a layperson's guide to understanding organizational culture.

or

> Schein (1999) provides a layperson's guide to understanding
>
> organizational culture.

When citing an English translation of a non-English work, include the author's name, the original date of publication, and the date of the English translation. For example:

> The French were not the first to make this observation (Foucault,
>
> 1969/1982).

When a reference contains a direct quotation, APA requires that a page number(s) be included in the parenthetical reference. The basic format for an APA parenthetical reference for a direct quotation is: (author's last name, comma, space, date, comma, space, "p." space, followed by the page number(s)). For example:

"The easiest level to observe when you go into an organization is

that of artifacts: what you see, hear, and feel as you hang around"

(Schein, 1999, p. 15).

APA RULE BOX 1

APA makes use of "p." to indicate a single page reference or "pp." to indicate that a quotation appears on more than one page of the cited material. Also note that the concluding punctuation appears at the end of an extended quotation BEFORE the parenthetical reference. In APA, no punctuation follows the parenthetical reference for an extended quotation.

The same rules apply when citing a direct quotation from a source with two authors. If the work cited has two authors, include the names of both authors each time the reference occurs in the text.

"Perhaps the most essential feature of human interaction is that it

involves adaptation" (White & Burgoon, 2001, p. 9).

If the work cited has three or more authors, include the names of all authors the first time a reference is made to the work. In subsequent references, include only the first author's name followed by "et al." (meaning "and others"), followed by a space and the date.

First reference:

"The assumption is that persons dishonest during the employment

interview will be dishonest on the job" (Mattson, Allen, Ryan, &

Miller, 2000, p. 148).

Each subsequent reference:

"Although further research is warranted, this study provides the

foundation on which to build a more complete understanding of

deception as both an interpersonal and an organizational

phenomenon" (Mattson et al., 2000, p. 155).

When a direct quotation exceeds 40 words in length, APA requires that the quotation be set off from the rest of the text. Introduce and cite the quotation as you would normally, omit the quotation marks, indent the entire quotation five spaces from the left margin, and type it in block form within the text. If the quotation exceeds 40 words in length and contains more than one paragraph, indent the first word of each subsequent paragraph five spaces from the new left margin. For example:

The social sciences are another matter.

> While theories about human behavior often cast their predictions in cause-and-effect terms, a certain humility on the part of the theorist is advisable. Even the best theory may only be able to talk in terms of probability and tendencies—not absolute certainty. (Griffin, 2000, p. 23)

Note that the punctuation appears at the end of the block quotation, not at the end of the citation for the quotation. Do not include any punctuation at the end of the citation for a block quotation.

When citing a single work by an author of two or more works with the same publication date in the text of your paper, include the suffixes a, b, c, and so forth after the year. You determine which reference gets which suffix by alphabetizing the references in your bibliography by the title of the work (because the author's name is the same for each reference) and then assigning "a" to the first, "b" to the second, and so on. Because suffixes are determined by alphabetical order, you may cite the reference with the "b" or "c" suffix in your paper before you cite the "a" suffix.

> In addition to examining the cultivation effect (Shrum, 1999b), the author also critiqued data collection methods (Shrum, 1999a), and analyzed the interaction of television programs and advertisements (Shrum, 1999c).

CITING SOURCES OBTAINED ELECTRONICALLY

The goal of any form of citation is to allow you or someone else to retrieve the information you have used in your manuscript. Your citation must be complete and allow others to retrace your steps in obtaining the information electronically. With electronic citations, punctuation and capitalization must be accurate in the address. Use standard APA rules and conventions for citing authors and sources discussed previously in this section, including rules for capitalization.

The June 2007 APA Style Guide to Electronic References includes the following major updates:

- Deletion of retrieval dates if the content is not going to be changed.
- Use of a DOI (Digital Object Identifier) instead of a URL—now available for some scholarly journals.
- Deletion of well-known database names unless the source is a hard-to-find book or other document of limited circulation.

In general these guidelines require electronic sources to use the following format that can be readily adapted to various forms of electronic material. Minor adaptations are necessary for electronic sources such as Web pages or electronic mail messages. Later in the chapter we provide examples of citations following this format:

Author's last name, first and middle initials. (Date of publication, revision, or

indicate n.d. for no date). Title of specific work. Complete DOI or Retrieved

from complete electronic address.

PRIMARY VERSUS SECONDARY SOURCES

To properly evaluate sources, you need to determine whether your supporting material is from a primary or a secondary source. Primary source material (direct) refers to research, information, or opinion as it was originally presented or published. Secondary source material (indirect) is a summary of research, information, or opinion prepared by someone other than the original creator. If someone conducts a study regarding the relationship between test apprehension and academic achievement and publishes the results of the study, that article is a primary source. If a student locates a copy of the printed article on test apprehension and academic achievement and uses information from the article in a course paper, the student's paper is a secondary source. When you cite a textbook, you often rely on a secondary source—the author of the textbook is summarizing the work done by others. You trust that the author of the text has read and analyzed primary source material and is accurately and objectively summarizing that material in the text.

CITING A SECONDARY SOURCE IN YOUR MANUSCRIPT

To document to the reader that you are relying upon secondary source material in your manuscript, identify the primary (direct) source and use "as cited in" preceding the secondary (indirect) source in which you found the material. In the list of references, only include the source you consulted (secondary source), not the primary source you are citing.

> Celia Green once wrote that, "The way to do research is to attack the facts at the point of greatest astonishment" (as cited in Reinhard, 2001, p. 183).

In this example Celia Green is the primary source and John Reinhard is the secondary source. In the list of references the citation would read:

Scholarly Writing 12

References

Reinhard, J. (2001). *Introduction to communication research* (3rd ed.). Boston: McGraw-Hill.

INDEX TO APA REFERENCE ENTRIES

SAMPLE APA ENTRIES

BOOKS

1. BOOK WITH ONE AUTHOR

Fairhurst, G. (2007). *Discursive leadership: In conversation with leadership psychology.* Thousand Oaks, CA: Sage.

Kanter, R. (2004). *Confidence: How winning streaks and losing streaks begin and end*. New York: Crown Business.

2. BOOK WITH TWO AUTHORS

Galanes, G., & Adams, K. (2007). *Effective group decisions: Theory and practice* (12th ed.). Boston: McGraw-Hill.

APA RULE BOX 4

How do I know which words to capitalize in the title of a book?

In book titles and subtitles, capitalize the first word of the title and of the subtitle, if any. All other words begin with a lowercase letter unless they are a capitalized term. Separate titles from subtitles with a colon. Include any other punctuation that is part of the title. Italicize the entire title, including the ending punctuation. For example:

Effective group discussion: Theory and practice.

---

3. BOOK WITH THREE OR MORE AUTHORS

Nelson, P. E., Pearson, J. C., & Titsworth, S. (2007). *Public speaking: A guide for the engaged communicator.* Boston: McGraw-Hill.

4. TWO OR MORE BOOKS BY THE SAME AUTHOR

Orbe, M. (2007). *Interracial communication* (2nd ed.). Thousand Oaks, CA: Sage.

Orbe, M. P. (1998). *Constructing co-cultural theory: An explication of culture, power, and communication.* Thousand Oaks, CA: Sage.

5. BOOK WITH AN EDITOR

May, S. (Ed.). (2006). *Case studies in organizational communication: Ethical perspectives and practices.* Thousand Oaks, CA: Sage.

6. BOOK WITH TWO EDITORS

Craig, R., & Muller, H. (Eds.). (2007). *Theorizing communication: Readings across traditions.* Thousand Oaks, CA: Sage.

Jablin, F. M., & Putnam, L. L. (Eds.). (2001). *The new handbook of organizational communication: Advances in theory, research, and methods.* Thousand Oaks, CA: Sage.

7. AN EDITION OTHER THAN THE FIRST

West, R., & Turner, L. *Introducing communication theory: Analysis and application* (3rd ed.). Boston: McGraw-Hill.

8. A WORK IN A BOOK

Miller, K. (2006). Communication as constructive. In G. Shepherd, J. John, & T. Striphas (Eds.), *Communication as: Perspectives on theory* (pp. 31-37). Thousand Oaks, CA: Sage.

APA RULE BOX 5

How do I know which words to capitalize in article and journal titles?

Capitalize the first word of an article title and subtitle, if any. Separate a title from its subtitle with a colon. For example:

Interpersonal deception: Communication apprehension as a contributing factor.

Give the journal title in full. Capitalize all nouns, pronouns, adjectives, and adverbs. Do not capitalize coordinating conjunctions (and, but, for, nor, or) or prepositions introducing phrases (of, before, in, to). Do not capitalize an article (a, an, the) unless it is the first word of a journal title. Italicize the title including the ending punctuation. For example:

Quarterly Journal of Speech.

---

9. A TRANSLATION

Aristotle. (1954). *The rhetoric* (W. R. Roberts, Trans.). New York: Modern Library. (Original work published 330 B.C.E.)

Foucault, M. (1982). *The archaeology of knowledge* (A. M. S. Smith, Trans.). New York: Pantheon Books. (Original work published 1969)

ARTICLES

The basic format for an article entry includes: author's name; date of publication; title of article; name of periodical; volume number; and page numbers.

10. ARTICLE WITH ONE AUTHOR

Abelman, R. (2007). Fighting the war on indecency: Mediating TV, Internet, and videogame usage among achieving and underachieving gifted children. *Roeper Review, 29,* 100-112.

Aubrey, J. S. (2007). The impact of sexually objectifying media exposure on negative body emotions and sexual self-perceptions: Investigating the mediating role of body self-consciousness. *Mass Communication & Society, 10,* 1-23.

11. ARTICLE WITH TWO AUTHORS

Barge, K., & Schlueter, D. (2004). Memorable messages and newcomer socialization. *Western Journal of Communication, 21,* 233-257.

Mazer, J. P., & Murphy, R. E. (2007). I'll see you on "Facebook": The effects of computer-mediated teacher self-disclosure on student motivation, affective learning, and classroom climate. *Communication Education, 56,* 1-17.

APA RULE BOX 6

When citing an article in a periodical, when do I use quotation marks and when do I italicize?

Quotation marks are never used in APA unless they are part of the punctuation of a title. Do not italicize article titles. Italicize book, journal, and film titles followed by a period. Italicize the period following the title. Italicize the commas before and after volume numbers in a periodical citation.

---

12. ARTICLE WITH THREE OR MORE AUTHORS

Allen, M., Bourhis J., Burrell N., & Mabry, E. (2002). Comparing student satisfaction with distance education to traditional classrooms in higher education: A meta-analysis. *American Journal of Distance Education, 16,* 83-89.

English, E., Llano, S., Mitchell, G., Morrison, C. E., Rief, J., & Woods, C. (2007). Debate as a weapon of mass destruction. *Communication & Critical/Cultural Studies, 4,* 221-225.

13. ARTICLE IN A MONTHLY OR BIMONTHLY PERIODICAL

Holland, R. J., & Potter, L. R. (2000, August). Customer vs. audience: When worlds collide. *Communication World, 17,* 15.

Make the right impact with technology. (2000, October). *Training, 37,* 1.

14. ARTICLE IN A WEEKLY OR BIWEEKLY PERIODICAL

Berman, D. (1998, November 2). Calling all raconteurs: Executive Communications Group holds executive storytelling seminars as a communication tool. *Business Week,* 6.

Slatalla, M. (2000, September 11). Brotherly love: A study suggests ways to rear siblings who will get along now—and for the rest of their lives. *Time, 156,* 122.

NEWSPAPERS

The basic format for a newspaper entry includes: author's name; date; article title; name of newspaper; and page.

15. SIGNED ARTICLE FROM A DAILY NEWSPAPER

Regan, T. (2007, October 17). Maybe e-mail isn't such a great idea, after all. *Christian Science Monitor,* p. 16.

16. UNSIGNED ARTICLE FROM A DAILY NEWSPAPER

Your career. (2007, October 14). *The Boston Globe,* p. V8.

17. SIGNED EDITORIAL FROM A DAILY NEWSPAPER

Young, Cathy. (2006, November 6). Radicalism in the deaf culture. *The Boston Globe,* p. A13.

18. UNSIGNED EDITORIAL FROM A DAILY NEWSPAPER

On the heights of excellence: Best school systems around the world avoid distractions such as faith-based funding. (2007, September 30). *The Toronto Star,* p. A25.

MANUSCRIPTS

19. UNPUBLISHED MANUSCRIPT

Adams, C. (2001). *Instructors' use of e-mail and student perceptions of immediacy.* Unpublished manuscript.

Striley, C. (2007). *The multiple realities of gifted children: Socially constructing the duality of privilege and marginalization.* Unpublished manuscript.

20. UNPUBLISHED PAPER PRESENTED AT A MEETING

Bohlman, D., & Harness, L. (2007, November). *Sunday morning drivers: A content analysis of topic choice and frequency in Sunday morning news shows.* Paper presented at the annual meeting of the National Communication Association, Chicago.

21. PERSONAL COMMUNICATIONS

Personal communications may include sources such as letters, memos, e-mail, messages from electronic bulletin boards, telephone conversations, interviews, and class lectures. Because they are not retrievable sources, APA does not include personal communications in the reference list. Instead, cite personal communications in the text only. Your instructor may give you specific instructions about citing certain nonretrievable sources such as interviews or class lectures. Absent any specific instructions, personal communications should be cited in the text as in these examples. Give the initials and surname of the communicator, and provide as exact a date as possible.

(J. B. Bourhis, personal communication, April 8, 2007)

(C. H. Adams, personal communication, January 28, 2007)

22. PUBLIC LECTURES

See the format for Personal Communications.

23. FILMS

The basic format for a film includes: director's name; date; film title; [Film]; place of production; and studio.

David, L. (Producer), Burns, S. Z. (Producer), Bender, L. (Producer), & Guggenheim, D. (Director). (2006). *An inconvenient truth* [Film]. Los Angeles: Paramount.

Schamus, J. (Producer), Hope, T. (Producer), & Lee, A. (Director). (1997). *The ice storm* [Film]. Los Angeles: Fox Searchlight Productions.

24. TELEVISION PROGRAMS

The basic format for a television program includes: program title; date of broadcast; and network. If the television program was produced locally, include place of origin and station. Include the episode or segment title if readily available.

CBS evening news. (2007, May 23). CBS.

CNN headline news. (2007, April 21). CNN.

25. RADIO BROADCASTS

The basic format for a radio broadcast includes: program title; date of broadcast; and network. If the radio broadcast was produced locally, replace network with place of origin and station.

All things considered. (2007, May 23). National Public Radio.

Morning edition. (2007, April 21). National Public Radio.

26. ENCYCLOPEDIA OR DICTIONARY

Bergman, P. G. (1993). Relativity. In *The New Encyclopedia Britannica*

(Vol. 26, pp. 501-508). Chicago: Encyclopedia Britannica.

ELECTRONIC SOURCES

27. INTERNET ARTICLE BASED ON A PRINT SOURCE

Many articles available online are exact duplicates from printed journals. In these cases, you may use the same basic format for referencing print articles, but if you have viewed only the electronic version of the article, you should add in brackets after the article title [Electronic version].

Allen, B. J. (2007). Theorizing communication and race [Electronic version].

Communication Monographs, 74, 256-258. doi:10.1080/03637750701393055

Litwin, A. H., & Hallstein, L. O. (2007). Shadows and silences: How women's

positioning and unspoken friendship rules in organizational settings cultivate

difficulties among some women at work [Electronic version]. *Women's*

Studies in Communication, 30, 111-142.

Many full-text articles available through online search engines and archives do not indicate page numbers, or in some other way alter the appearance of the original print version. If the online version has been changed in some way from the print version, you also must add the date you retrieved the document and the DOI or URL.

Dahlberg, L. (2001). The Internet and democratic discourse: Exploring the

prospects of online deliberative forums extending the public sphere.

Information, Communication, and Society, 4(4), 615-633. doi:

10.1080/13691180110097030

Fundamentalism in the modern world. (2002, March-April). *Sojourners.*

Retrieved from http://www.sojo.net/magazine/index.cfm/

action/sojourners/issue/soj0203/article/020310.html

28. ARTICLE IN AN INTERNET-ONLY JOURNAL OR PERIODICAL

Paolillo, J. (1999). The virtual speech community: Social network and language

variation on IRC [Online exclusive]. *Journal of Computer-Mediated*

Communication, 4(4). Retrieved from http://jcmc.indiana.edu/vol4/issue4/

paolillo.html

Dark, D. (2004, March 11). Celebrate the Simpsons [Online exclusive]. *Relevant.*

Retrieved from http://www.relevantmagazine.com/article.php?sid=914

29. MULTIPAGE DOCUMENT CREATED BY PRIVATE ORGANIZATION, NO DATE

When different pages of a document have different URLs, provide a URL that links
to the home page for the document. Date is included below because document may
have changed. Use n.d. (no date) when a publication date is not available.

National Communication Association (n.d.). *Assessment resources.* Retrieved

April 11, 2007, from http://www.natcom.org

30. STAND-ALONE DOCUMENT, NO AUTHOR IDENTIFIED, NO DATE

Critical issues in education and technology (n.d.). Retrieved from

http://www.ctf-fce.ca/e/what/restech/critical.htm

31. E-MAIL

E-mail sent from one individual to another should be cited as a personal
communication (see p. 66).

32. ELECTRONIC COPY OF AN ARTICLE OR ABSTRACT RETRIEVED FROM A DATABASE

Many online databases allow access to full-text versions of articles from many different journals and other periodicals. When referencing articles accessed through such databases, follow the format appropriate for the type of work retrieved (e.g., a journal article, a newspaper article). The database name is no longer a necessary element of the reference, with the exception of hard-to-find books and other documents of limited circulation. If you do include the database name in a reference, do not include the database URL.

Hubbard, A. S. E. (2001). Conflict between relationally uncertain romantic

partners: The influence of relational responsiveness and empathy.

Communication Monographs, 68(4), 400-414. Abstract retrieved from

http://www.cios.org/www/abstract.htm

Samter, W. (2002). How gender and cognitive complexity influence the provision

of emotional support: A study of indirect effects. *Communication Reports,*

15(2), 5-16. Retrieved from http://esearch.epnet.com/

Sharos, D. (2002, April 11). Where promotions are par for the course. *Chicago*

Tribune. Retrieved from http://www.chicagotribune.com

33. ONLINE DISCUSSION GROUPS AND ELECTRONIC MAILING LISTS

In general, online discussion sources should be referenced only if they have scholarly value and are retrievable. If messages are not in an accessible archive, they should be cited as a personal communication (see p. 66), similar to e-mail.

Kumaschow, P. (2007, March 31). Virtual journeys. Message posted to

http://groups.yahoo.com/group/onlineeducationandtraining/message/791

Kurylo, A. (2007, November 27). Sound familiar? Message posted to

COMGRADS electronic mailing list, archived at http://www.cios.org/

mailboxes/comgrads/11271155.106

PREPARING THE LIST OF REFERENCES

The list of references appears at the end of the paper. Begin the list on a new page and number each page. Continue with the page numbers of the text. The title "References" appears centered at the top of the page. The title "Reference" is used if there is only one reference in the paper. Double-space between the title and the first entry. Use a hanging indent for each entry (i.e., the first line is flush left and subsequent lines are indented 5–7 spaces). Double-space the entire list, both between and within entries.

Arrange the entries in the list of references in alphabetical order by the author's last name. If the author's name is unknown, alphabetize the entry by the first word of the title other than "A," "An," and "The." "The Recession Is Coming" would be alphabetized under "R" in the list of references. When ordering several entries by the same author, arrange the entries chronologically from earliest to latest. When ordering entries with the same first author and different second authors, arrange the entries alphabetically by second author. Single-author entries precede multiple-author entries beginning with the same surname. When listing multiple works by the same author with the same date of publication, arrange your entries on the reference page alphabetically by title ignoring "a, and, the" when they appear as the first word in a title.

Television Viewing 8

References

Shrum, L. J. (1999a). *The effect of data-collection method on the cultivation effect: Implications for the heuristic processing model of cultivation effects*. Paper presented at the meeting of the International Communication Association, San Francisco, CA.

Shrum, L. J. (1999b). The relationship of television viewing with attitude strength and extremity: Implications for the cultivation effect. *Media Psychology, 1,* 3-25.

Shrum, L. J. (1999c). Television and persuasion: Effects of the programs between the ads. *Psychology and Marketing, 16,* 119-140.

My Paper 8

References

Craig, R. T. (1995).

Craig, R. T., & Tracy, K. (1995).

APPENDIX A
Model Paper Following APA Guidelines

Running head: MATERIAL WORLD

In APA, pagination includes a short abbreviation of the title and the page number on every page of the manuscript, including the title page.

Living in a Material World:

Origins and Implications of Objectification Theory

Katie Margavio Striley

Missouri State University

The running head only appears on the title page of the manuscript and is used by journal editors for publication purposes. Note the unusual use of upper- and lowercase letters. Students frequently make mistakes in typing the running head.

Include title, your first and last name, and your school affiliation, all double spaced using upper- and lowercase letters.

Living in a Material World:

Origins and Implications of Objectification Theory

Women and men are continually inundated with media images of gender stereotypes and sexuality (Bolls & Aubrey, 2005). Media, whether subtly or blatantly, send messages to women and men about "proper" ways to look and act. These messages are apparent in cartoons (Al-Mahadin, 2003), movies (Bain, 2003), television (Monro, 2005), sports media (Messner & de Oca, 2005), MTV (Gow, 1996), magazines (Nelson & Paek, 2005), and advertisements (Nelson & Paek, 2005; Rohlinger, 2002). After a lifetime of this deluge of gender role messages, most individuals come to view themselves in terms of their gender (Allen, 2004). Humans are born into a coded world that is difficult to escape. The current paper seeks to explore how individuals reproduce cultural gender stereotypes through the lens of objectification theory (Fredrickson & Roberts, 1997).

Objectification Theory: You Are What You See

The conceptual foundation of objectification theory can be found in Gerbner's (1969) cultivation theory (Aubrey, 2005a). This theory argues that media shape the way individuals view the world; therefore, repeatedly viewing certain patterns of media communication will produce certain perceptions of reality (Reber & Chang, 2000). Objectification theory posits that media images objectify women (Fredrickson & Roberts, 1997); this causes members of society to come to view women as objects (Aubrey, 2005a; Strelan & Hargreaves, 2005b). This objectified view, then, coaxes women into objectifying themselves (Sinclair, 2006). The process of self-objectification starts at a young age (Murnen, Smolak, Mills, & Good, 2003), and cycles of objectification are then created (Strelan & Hargreaves, 2005b). This process must be understood in greater depth than this, however.

Paginate every page of the manuscript.

Indent each new paragraph 1/2 inch or approximately five spaces. Double-space all text.

In APA all text citations should include year of publication or access.

Do not use full justification, use a ragged right-hand margin.

To begin with, media promote women to look a certain way (Monro, 2005). "American culture sends a powerful signal to women—that only the beautiful and the thin are valued and loved, catalyzing an American ideal of female body image where thinness is a sign of success, health, and being in charge of your life" (Hesse-Biber, Leavey, & Quinn, 2006, p. 208). "Media emphasize ideal bodies by visually focusing on bodies and presenting bodies in increasingly gender-typed and objectified ways" (Aubrey, 2003, p. 3). Objectification is "the experience of being treated *as a body* (or collection of body parts) valued predominately for its use to (or consumption by) others" (Fredrickson & Roberts, 1997, p. 174). These images are inherent within most of American media (Aubrey, 2003). They can be as blatant as displaying lone body parts with no head pictured (Fredrickson & Roberts, 1997), to as subtle as displaying a woman in a "mental drift" (Rohlinger, 2002, p. 67) with a male gazing at her (Aubrey, 2003; Slater & Tiggemann, 2002). Fredrickson and Roberts argue that "confrontation with these images, then, is virtually unavoidable in American culture" (p. 177).

Objectification theory argues that girls and women are affected in a very real way by media objectification; they are coaxed to "adopt a peculiar view of self" (Fredrickson & Roberts, 1997, p. 177). At some level, the media milieu of objectification pushes women to "treat *themselves* as objects to be looked at and evaluated" (p. 177). "The more positive the evaluation, the more likely a woman is to be valued by others" (Strelan & Hargreaves, 2005b, p. 707). This encourages women to "define the self in terms of how it appears to others, rather than performance, achievement, or emotional well-being" (Aubrey, 2005b, p. 5).

Observe 1 inch margins on all sides.

In APA use the ampersand sign "&" instead of "and" in the in-text citation.

In most cases, punctuate at the end of the citation, not at the end of the material cited.

In APA use "p." for page or "pp." for inclusive pages in the citation.

Note the comma that goes after the author's name and before the year of publication.

Objectification theory has been primarily concerned with women, because cultural standards of attractiveness have traditionally been more important for women than for men (Calogero, 2004; Fredrickson & Roberts, 1997). Women consistently report higher levels of self-objectification than men (Aubrey, 2003; Roberts & Gettman, 2004). However, there has been a growing emphasis on men's physical appearance in mainstream media (Rohlinger, 2002; Tager, Good, & Bauber, 2006).

Fitting Men Into the Equation

Objectification theory specifically states that women are affected by objectification more than men (Fredrickson & Roberts, 1997); therefore, men have not been studied nearly as much as women, with regard to objectification (Roberts & Gettman, 2004; Tager, et al., 2006). However, some scholars have begun to notice an increase in male objectification (Spitzer, Henderson, & Zivian, 1999). Men have recently been put on display, and media portrayals of males are becoming increasingly objectified and sexualized (Rohlinger, 2002). Men are becoming increasingly concerned with their bodies (Strelan & Hargreaves, 2005a). Strelan and Hargreaves are some of the first scholars who applied objectification theory to men; they believe the basic tenets of objectification theory can apply to both genders. Strelan and Hargreaves argue that men are also beginning to believe that, in order to be valued by society, they must attain a certain body image. The introduction of terms like "metrosexual," a slang term for a man "who spends a great deal of time and money on appearance" (Aubrey, 2005b, p. 7), points to this growing trend of male objectification.

Harmful Effects of Objectification

Objectification theory asserts that a number of harmful effects occur when women or men objectify themselves. "This tendency to self-objectify activates a process in which people are likely to experience negative health outcomes" (Aubrey, 2003, p. 3). These negative effects can include low sexual esteem (Wiederman & Hurst, 1998), sexual dysfunction (Aubrey, 2003; Fredrickson & Roberts, 1997), anxiety and shame (Fredrickson & Roberts, 1997; Greenleaf & McGreer, 2006; Slater & Tiggemann, 2002; Tiggemann & Lynch, 2001), depression (Fredrickson & Roberts, 1997), body dissatisfaction (Monro, 2005; Strelan & Hargreaves, 2005a), lower self-esteem (Hesse-Biber, et al., 2006), eating disorders (Hesse-Biber, et al., 2006; Greenleaf & McGreer, 2006), and lower performance (Quinn, Kallen, Twenge, & Fredrickson, 2006). Hesse-Biber and colleagues point out that anorexia is one of the few psychiatric disorders with a significant mortality rate.

It should be noted that effects like these have generally been found for women, whereas men seem to be less affected (Murnen, et al., 2003; Strelan & Hargreaves, 2005a). This may be because male objectification is less prevalent in American society (Strelan & Hargreaves, 2005a). Although with male eating disorders on the rise (Braun, Sunday, Huang, & Halmi, 1999), and an increase in male body dissatisfaction (Tager, et al., 2006), effects of objectification on males may become more pronounced in the coming years.

Female and male objectification can be seen in many aspects of American society. As the United States becomes more of a material world, objectification begins to rise. Initially, only females were studied in regard to this theory of self-objectification, but as American society has become

---

Note that the heading is typed in upper and lower case, italicized, and set flush left.

"et al." is a Latin abbreviation for "and others." Use to substitute for a list of names in a citation.

increasingly more superficial, males have become objectified as well. Americans are living in a material world and are becoming even more materialistic. If these trends continue, female and male objectification will continue to rise, and negative repercussions will be felt even more strongly.

Material World 7

References

Allen, B. J. (2004). *Difference matters: Communicating social identity*. Long Grove, IL: Waveland Press.

Al-Mahadin, S. (2003). Gender representations and stereotypes in cartoons: A Jordanian case study. *Feminist Media Studies, 3,* 131-151.

Aubrey, J. S. (2003). Investigating the role of self-objectification in the relationship between media exposure and sexual self-perceptions. Paper presented at International Communication Association Annual Meeting.

Aubrey, J. S. (2005a). Effects of sexually objectifying media on self-objectification and body surveillance in undergraduates: Results of two-year panel study. Paper presented at International Communication Association Annual Meeting.

Aubrey, J. S. (2005b). Examining longitudinal relations between exposure to lad-genre media and undergraduates' body self-consciousness. Paper presented at International Communication Association Annual Meeting.

Bain, A. L. (2003). White Western teenage girls and urban space: Challenging Hollywood's representations. *A Journal of Feminist Geography, 10(3),* 197-214.

Bolls, P., & Aubrey, J. S. (2005). The effects of priming self-objectification on college women's encoding of television advertisements. Paper presented at the International Communication Association Annual Meeting, New York.

Braun, D. L., Sunday, S. R., Huang, A., & Halmi, K. A. (1999). More males seek treatment for eating disorders. *International Journal of Eating Disorders, 25,* 415-424.

Calogero, R. M. (2004). A test of objectification theory: The effect of the male gaze on appearance concerns in college women. *Psychology of Women Quarterly, 28,* 16-21.

Fredrickson, B. L., & Roberts, T. A. (1997). Objectification theory: Toward understanding women's lived experiences and mental health risks. *Psychology of Women Quarterly, 21,* 173-206.

Gerbner, G. (1969). Toward "cultural indicators": The analysis of mass mediated message systems. *Communication Review, 17,* 137-148.

Greenleaf, C., & McGreer, R. (2006). Disordered eating attitudes and self-objectification among physically active and sedentary female college students. *The Journal of Psychology, 140,* 187-198.

Gow, J. (1996). Reconsidering gender roles on MTV: Depictions in the most popular music videos of the early 1990s. *Communication Reports, 9,* 152-161.

Hesse-Biber, S., Leavey, P., & Quinn, C. E. (2006). The mass marketing of disordered eating and eating disorders: The social psychology of women, thinness and culture. *Women's Studies International Forum, 29,* 208-224.

Messner, M. A., & de Oca, J. M. (2005). The male consumer as loser: Beer and liquor ads in mega sports media events. *Journal of Women in Culture & Society, 30,* 1879-1909.

Monro, F. (2005). Media-portrayed idealized images, body shame, and appearance anxiety. *International Journal of Eating Disorders, 38,* 85-90.

Murnen, S. K., Smolak, L., Mills, J. A., & Good, L. (2003). Thin, sexy women and strong, muscular men: Grade-school children's responses to objectified images of women and men. *Sex Roles, 49,* 427-437.

Nelson, M. R., & Paek, H. (2005). Cross-cultural differences in sexual advertising content in a transnational women's magazine. *Sex Roles, 53,* 371-383.

Quinn, D. M., Kallen, R. W., Twenge, J. M., & Fredrickson, B. L. (2006). The disruptive effect of self-objectification on performance. *Psychology of Women Quarterly, 30,* 59-64.

Reber, B. H., & Chang, Y. (2000). Assessing cultivation theory and public health model for crime reporting. *Newspaper Research Journal, 21(4),* 99-112.

Roberts, T. A., & Gettman, J. Y. (2004). Mere exposure: Gender differences in the negative effects of priming a state of self-objectification. *Sex Roles, 51,* 17-27.

Rohlinger, D. A. (2002). Eroticizing men: Cultural influences on advertising and male objectification. *Sex Roles, 46,* 61-74.

Sinclair, S. L. (2006). Object lessons: A theoretical and empirical study of objectified body consciousness in women. *Journal of Mental Health and Counseling, 28,* 48-68.

Slater, A., & Tiggemann, M. (2002). A test of objectification theory in adolescent girls. *Sex Roles, 46,* 343-349.

Spitzer, B. L., Henderson, K. A., & Zivian, M. T. (1999). Gender differences in population versus media body sizes: A comparison over four decades. *Sex Roles, 40,* 545-565.

Strelan, P., & Hargreaves, D. (2005a). Reasons for exercise and body esteem: Men's responses to self-objectification. *Sex Roles, 53,* 495-503.

Strelan, P., & Hargreaves, D. (2005b). Women who objectify other women: The vicious circle of objectification? *Sex Roles, 52,* 707-712.

Tiggemann, M., & Lynch, J. E. (2001). Body image across the life span in adult women: The role of self-objectification. *Developmental Psychology, 37(2),* 243-253.

Tager, D., Good, G. E., & Bauber, J. (2006). Our bodies, ourselves revisited: Male body image and psychological well-being. *International Journal of Men's Health, 5,* 228-237.

Wiedermann, M. W., & Hurst, S. W. (1998). Body size, physical attractiveness, and body image among young adult women: Relationships to sexual experience and sexual esteem. *The Journal of Sex Research, 35(3),* 272-281.

APPENDIX B
Model Annotated Bibliography in APA Style

Running head: SYMBOLIC CONVERGENCE THEORY

Symbolic Convergence Theory:

An Annotated Bibliography

Jane Doe

Missouri State University

In APA, pagination includes a short abbreviation of the title and the page number on every page of the manuscript, including the title page.

The running head only appears on the title page of the manuscript and is used by journal editors for publication purposes. Note the unusual use of upper- and lowercase letters. Students frequently make mistakes in typing the running head.

Include title, your first and last name, and your school affiliation, all double-spaced using upper and lower case.

Symbolic Convergence Theory:

An Annotated Bibliography

Bormann, E. (1972). Fantasy and rhetorical visions: The rhetorical criticism of social reality. *Quarterly Journal of Speech, 58(4),* 396-408.

> The focus of this theoretical essay is threefold. Bormann first seeks to articulate the interrelation between small group communication and rhetorical theory. He ascertains that small groups create rhetorical visions in much the same way as when individuals participate in public address or mass communication. Bormann argues that small group fantasizing is similar to the fantasizing instigated by mass media and rhetoric. Second, Bormann addresses the creation of fantasy themes and how these themes chain out to others. This process occurs when individuals create dramas and share these dramas with others; this occurs frequently in religion and politics. These interactions are not limited to small groups; they occur in large groups as well. Finally, Bormann briefly outlines the fantasy theme analysis. This is a method that allows for viewing the process of fantasy theme chaining.

Bormann, E. (1973). The Eagleton Affair: A fantasy theme analysis. *Quarterly Journal of Speech, 59(2),* 143-160.

> This analysis focuses on the 1972 United States presidential campaign. Bormann performs a fantasy theme analysis in order to discover the rhetorical visions defined and embodied by political parties during this election cycle. Bormann particularly focuses on the drama surrounding presidential candidate McGovern and his running mate, Eagleton. McGovern and Eagleton lost control of their "story," and this ultimately cost them the election. Alleged stories about Eagleton's drinking problem and his

Center the title of the manuscript using upper- and lowercase letters. Double-space to the first line of the manuscript.

Note that in APA, the italicizing of a title includes the punctuation at the end of the title.

APA makes use of a "hanging indent" format for references. The first line of each reference is set flush left while each subsequent line is indented five spaces.

bouts of nervousness were chained out to the American

public, and both McGovern and Eagleton began to look

like villains in the eyes of the public.

Bormann, E. (1982). The symbolic convergence theory of

communication: Applications and implications for teachers

and consultants. *Journal of Applied Communication*

Research, 10(1), 50-62.

    In this theoretical piece, Bormann presents the struc-

ture of symbolic convergence theory, defines key terms

utilized in the theory, and discusses practical applications.

Bormann particularly focuses on how fantasy theme

chaining helps to create culture and fosters a collective

consciousness among group members. Bormann explains

that a fantasy theme analysis can be helpful in uncover-

ing hidden problems in organizations that members did

not know were occurring. Finally, he points out that a fan-

tasy theme analysis can very easily be used to analyze an

organization, in politics, and when looking at mass media.

Cragan, J. F., & Sheilds, D. C. (1992). The use of

symbolic convergence theory in corporate strategic planning:

A case study. *Journal of Applied Communication Research,*

20(2), 199-218.

    This study applies symbolic convergence theory to the

context of corporate planning. The authors did a case

study of how a specific corporation attempted to create a

shared symbolic reality. The authors point out that any-

thing a corporation does can be explained with symbolic

convergence theory; corporations decide on a name, a

reputation, a corporate saga, etc. Corporations use sym-

bols and try to chain these symbols out so that a collective

reality is created in whatever image the corporation

desires.

Paginate every page of the manuscript; double-space throughout.

Observe 1 inch margins on all sides of the manuscript.

Endres, T. G. (1997). Father-daughter dramas: A q-investigation of rhetorical visions. *Journal of Applied Communication, 25,* 317-340.

This study assessed the rhetorical visions surrounding father-daughter relationships. The study was conducted in two phases. Phase I examined academic and popular press rhetoric surrounding narratives of the father-daughter relationship. Four rhetorical visions emerged: the knight in shining armor, the buddy, the authoritarian, and the shadow. Phase II of the study utilized a Q-sort methodology to test the resonance of these rhetorical visions with real-life daughters. Forty-five adult daughters were given a Q-sort card deck and ranked each card on a "most like me" to "least like me" scale. A QUANAL revealed the adult daughters tended to agree with the rhetorical visions found in rhetoric. Additionally, Endres stresses the importance of father-daughter relationships on girls' senses of self.

Koester, J. (1982). The Machiavellian princess: Rhetorical dramas for women managers. *Communication Quarterly, 30(3),* 165-172.

A fantasy theme analysis was performed on women's self-help books to determine dominant rhetorical visions about female managers. Koester found that women are forced to control the impact of their gender in a Machiavellian way. Women are told to balance negative stereotypes, and maintain femininity at the same time. Additionally, many of these books tell women that nothing will impede their success except their own negative attitude; however, this may not be the truth in the real world. Ultimately, Koester concludes that these books are contradictory and provide women with an incomplete vision.

Putnam, L. L., Van Hoevan, S. A., & Bullis, C. A. (1991). The role of rituals and fantasy themes in teachers' bargaining. *Western Journal of Speech Communication, 55,* 85-103.

The authors observed the teacher-administrator negotiation sessions of two school districts and employed a multi-method approach to ascertain the role of fantasies in the bargaining process. The researchers sought to understand how these teachers and administrators created and framed reality in their sessions. Both school districts identified heroes and villains during their negotiations and viewed each other as opponents in conflict. Ultimately, the different visions between teachers and administrators were the source of conflict and misunderstanding.

Schrag, R. L., Hudson, R. A., & Bernabo, L. M. (1981). Television's new humane collectivity. *Western Journal of Speech Communication, 45,* 1-12.

This study employed a fantasy theme analysis to uncover the major rhetorical visions that are created in primetime television. The heroes, villains, and plotlines of a number of television programs were analyzed. The authors argue that a positive rhetorical vision is emerging. The fantasy themes they found included recognizing the importance of significant others in life, the importance of forming alliances, and the importance of personhood. The combination of these, they argue, creates the vision of a new humane collectivity. The vision is meant to inspire members of society to work together, love each other, and act humanely.

Stone, J. F. (2002). Using symbolic convergence theory to discern and segment motives for enrolling in professional master's degree programs. *Communication Quarterly, 50(2),* 227-243.

In an attempt to understand a steep decline in graduate enrollment, a fantasy theme analysis was completed to uncover rhetorical visions underpinning students' decisions to enroll in the program. This analysis was completed over a four-year period by surveying hundreds of students. Several visions emerged, including the idea that students wanted high-quality universities because they believed these had better programs, and they wanted small campuses because they believed this led to better opportunities. Stone discusses what implications this may have on recruitment and retention of graduate students.

Vasquez, G. M. (1993). A homo narran paradigm for public relations: Combining Bormann's symbolic convergence theory and Grunig's situational theory of publics. *Journal of Public Relations Research, 5(3),* 201-216.

This article combines SCT and situational theory to create the *homo narran* paradigm, a public relations model. Vasquez spends a good deal of time reporting on what SCT is, how it came to be created, and the history of its uses. Vasquez also discusses practical applications of SCT and provides a model of what a fantasy theme analysis may look like. He combines these ideas with situational theory, which sheds light on how to identify relevant publics and tailor messages to these publics. Ultimately, the article presents a theory that addresses how to get certain publics to collectively create the same reality through interpreting and sharing symbols.

APPENDIX C
Model Journal Critique in APA Style

Sex and Social Support   1

Running head: SEX AND SOCIAL SUPPORT

Sex Differences and Similarities in the Communication of

Social Support:

A Journal Article Critique

Michelle Redepenning

Minnesota State University Moorhead

In APA, pagination includes a short abbreviation of the title and the page number on every page of the manuscript, including the title page.

The running head only appears on the title page of the manuscript and is used by journal editors for publication purposes. Note the unusual use of upper- and lowercase letters. Students frequently make mistakes in typing the running head.

Include title, your first and last name, and your school affiliation, all double-spaced using upper- and lowercase letters.

Sex Differences and Similarities in the

Communication of Social Support:

A Journal Article Critique

Source

Goldsmith, D., & Dun, S. (1997). Sex differences and

similarities in the communication of social support. *Journal

of Social and Personal Relationships, 14*, 317–337.

Purpose

Previous research suggests that because men and women

represent different cultures, they may respond differently

when communicating support. According to such

perspectives, men and women communicate differently in

interpersonal relationships and such differences are

consistent with instrumental versus expressive roles. Despite

limited supporting evidence, these are widely accepted views

in both public and academic discourse. The purpose of this

study was to observe whether, in fact, differences exist in the

communication of social support among men and women. To

do this, the authors examined differences in length,

frequency, and communication styles used by men and

women in response to scenarios requiring the

communication of social support.

Rationale

Ideologies about sex differences in the communication

of social support are reflected and reinforced in the

discourses of popular culture; yet, there is little empirical

data upon which belief systems are based. The authors

attempt to challenge the foundation upon which such

assumptions rest. In addition to making theoretical

contributions to existing literature on gender

communication and social support, the project has

practical value. Common assumptions that men

Paginate every page of the manuscript.

Center the title of the manuscript using upper- and lowercase letters. Double-space to the first line of the manuscript.

When citing the article you are critiquing, follow the rules for citing a source as it would appear in a list of Works Cited or References.

Do not use full justification, use a ragged right-hand margin.

For most student papers you will use two types of headings: level 1 and level 2. Level 1 headings are centered in the page. Level 2 headings are flush to the left margin and italicized. Use upper- and lowercase letters for all headings. Do not use boldface. There are three level 2 headings on this page of the journal critique.

Indent the first line of each new paragraph 1/2 inch or approximately five spaces from the left margin.

Observe 1 inch margins on all sides of the manuscript.

only provide instrumental support and women only provide emotional support, if inaccurate, may seriously limit individuals' perceptions of their communication abilities and choices. Additionally, even if males and females differ in the amount and type of support provided in relationships, both genders can learn how to provide instrumental and expressive support.

Methodology

The authors empirically tested ten hypotheses based on previous research:

H1: Men's responses will be shorter than women's responses;

H2: Men and women will not differ in the frequency of responses that discuss actions to solve the problem or alleviate negative emotions;

H3: Women's responses will discuss the other's problems and emotional reactions more frequently than will men's responses;

H4: Men will deny problems and emotions more often than women;

H5: Men's responses will discuss actions more often than problems or emotions;

H6: Women's responses will discuss problems and emotions more often than actions;

H7: Men and women will exhibit different patterns of relative frequency of talk about problems, emotions, and actions;

H8: For men, denying problems and emotions will be more common than other ways of talking about problems and emotions;

H9: For women, denying problems and emotions will be less common than other ways of talking about problems and emotions; and

H10: Men and women will exhibit different patterns of relative frequency of denying or not denying problems and emotions.

One hundred undergraduates, 49 men and 51 women between the ages of 18 and 22 years, were asked to read and respond to nine situations in which another person disclosed some problem and appeared to be upset about that problem. Responses were tape-recorded and transcribed. To analyze the data, the authors used a coding system in which students' responses were categorized as problem-focused, emotion-focused, or action-focused.

Following the initial coding, authors analyzed problem- and emotion-focused responses to determine "whether or not a speaker was verbally denying or minimizing a problem or emotional reaction" (p. 325). After coding of transcripts, the authors relied primarily on ANOVA procedures and t-tests, including follow-up procedures when appropriate, to test the hypotheses about gender differences in the communication of support.

Results

The results of the study found little support for past claims that men and women represent different cultures and therefore communicate differently when offering support. Consistent with H1, researchers found that women provided significantly longer responses than men. In addition, the length of responses did vary by situation. Researchers discovered a contradiction to H2 predicting that men and women will not differ in the amount of action-focused support. In fact, women's communication included significantly more action-focused responses than men. H3 was partially supported in that women's responses were significantly more emotion-focused than men's. Women and men did not differ in the number of problem-focused responses.

Since men and women differed in length of responses, researchers controlled for that difference in subsequent hypothesis-testing. Additional tests revealed that men and women did not differ in their responses in terms of emotion-focus or action-focus; however, men overwhelmingly focused their responses on the problem. H4 was partially supported as well, indicating women and men differed significantly in the denial of the problem, but did not differ in the denial of emotions. H5 was supported in that men provide more action-focus than emotion-focus responses. Surprisingly, both men and women frequently communicated both problem- and action-focused responses more often than emotion-focused responses.

Contrary to H8, men were more likely to respond in ways that would not deny or minimize experiences rather than engage in the denial of a problem or emotion. Women were also more likely to talk about problems and emotions without denying them, thus supporting H9. Thus, contrary to H10, men and women were roughly similar in terms of not denying a problem or emotion in their communication of social support.

The overall conclusions suggest that there is little evidence in support of dominant stereotypes that women typically provide empathic emotional support and men typically provide instrumental advice and aid. In short, these results suggest that sex differences in the communication of social support are exceedingly small and the similarities between the sexes are substantial.

Evaluation

This study has broad theoretical scope in the sense that the results provide a base from which to question assumptions about gendered communication in general as well as the gendered communication of social support specifically. The authors challenge future researchers to focus on similarities across situations and genders as well as potential communication differences.

One potential weakness of this study is the sample of participants. First, the participants were not randomly selected. Additionally, the sample included mostly white college students between the ages of 18 and 22 years. Most participants were communication majors most likely educated in sex differences and gender stereotypes. I question whether the same data collection process would have yielded similar results with a more diverse population—an audience consisting of people with varying ages, races, religions, geographic locations, education levels, and socioeconomic statuses. Future research designs would have more external validity if the sample was more diverse and participants were selected using more rigorous methods. The generalizability of the current results are limited by the sample.

A second potential weakness is the difficulty in receiving genuine and accurate feedback from respondents. Rather than analyzing the participants' verbal and nonverbal behaviors when engaged in naturally occurring dialogue, participants listened to hypothetical situations and shared their hypothetical responses with a tape recorder. It may be difficult to determine whether responses are consistent with how people would actually communicate in everyday situations requiring social support. Research designs would have more internal validity if they were to observe participants during naturally occurring face-to-face encounters with a "live" person experiencing the need for social and/or emotional support. Of course, it is difficult to obtain access to such interactions for research purposes.

From a heuristic perspective, this study has merit. Because mainstream culture perpetuates the ideology that women communicate primarily emotional support and men communicate primarily instrumental support, research that provides alternative ways of thinking is critical to truly understanding patterns of gendered communication. There are also practical implications for a program of research on the study of sex differences and similarities. Most self-help books and other artifacts throughout our culture highlight extreme gender differences and styles of communication. Collectively, this discourse potentially influences not only dominant perceptions of gender differences but also the way in which men and women communicate with family, friends, and in the workplace. If indeed future research shows that women and men communicate similarly when providing support, such findings would have profound implications for popular discourse on gender differences.

APPENDIX D
Model Research Report in APA Style

Running head: ORGANIZATIONAL LECTURE CUES

In APA, pagination includes a short abbreviation of the title and the page number on every page of the manuscript, including the title page.

The Effects of Organizational Lecture Cues on Student

Notetaking and Cognitive Learning

Harold W. Smith

Northern Central University

Russell D. Smith

Midwestern State University

The running head only appears on the title page of the manuscript and is used by journal editors for publication purposes. Note the unusual use of upper- and lowercase letters. Students frequently make mistakes in typing the running head.

Include title, your first and last name, and your school affiliation, all double-spaced using upper- and lowercase letters.

Abstract

This experimental study tested the effect of teachers' use of organizational lecture cues and students' ($N = 60$) notetaking on achievement. Results of the experiment indicated that (a) teacher organizational lecture cues and student notetaking each boosted achievement and (b) organizational cues and organization of students' notes are significant predictors of achievement. Based on these and other findings, it was concluded that teachers' use of organizational cues coupled with student notetaking results in greater student learning.

"Abstract" is centered at the top of the page in upper- and lowercase letters.

Note that the first word in the abstract is not indented 1/2 inch as are new paragraphs throughout the manuscript.

An abstract is a very concise statement that summarizes for the reader the content of the manuscript. Abstracts are most commonly associated with the reporting of empirical study and are not common for the typical student paper.

The Effects of Organizational Lecture Cues on Student

Notetaking and Cognitive Learning

A fact of life for many college students is that notetaking remains an essential ingredient for academic success. This fact is partly due to the observation that the lecture method remains a "sacred cow" among most college and university instructors (Carrier, Williams, & Dalagard, 1988). Because college instructors view lecturing as a central aspect of their professional identity, this format of instruction has become common throughout college and university classrooms, even in an era championing group-based and active learning teaching strategies (McKeachie, 1999). Although vernacular descriptions of the lecture situation assume students are merely passive receptors of knowledge, such descriptions may be overly pessimistic. In fact, students quickly learn that active listening behaviors, including taking notes, are required for success.

The problem with this lecture–notetaking relationship is twofold. First, not all students are equal in their notetaking skills. Although students believe that notetaking is both important and common in the college setting (Carrier et al., 1988; Palmatier & Bennett, 1974), they do not always take effective notes. "In a lecture situation some students (using shorthand) seem to want to record everything said by the lecturer," observed Hartley and Davies (1978), "others pick and choose relevant points, and others indulge in a certain amount of doodling whilst they listen" (p. 207). This variance in notetaking skill (or effort) results in some students having more complete notes than others. In general, upper level students tend to take more notes than lower level

---

Paginate every page of the manuscript.

Center the title of the manuscript using upper- and lowercase letters. Double-space to the first line of the manuscript.

Do not use full justification; use a ragged right-hand margin.

Note the use of the ampersand sign "&" in the Carrier et al. citation instead of "and." This is a distinguishing characteristic of APA style.

In the text of the paper use "and," not the ampersand.

Indent the first line of each new paragraph 1/2 inch or approximately five spaces from the left margin.

Observe 1 inch margins on all sides of the manuscript.

students (Kiewra, 1984). Moreover, research by Locke (1977) indicates that students record approximately 60% of the lecture points, and that students record more notes from material written on the board (88%) than material presented orally (52%). Other research has found that the amount of lecture information recorded by students is much lower, somewhere between 30% and 40% (Kiewra, 1984).

> A distinguishing characteristic of APA style is to include the date of publication or access in the in-text citation.

The problem of inadequate and varied skill in notetaking is compounded by the importance of notetaking on students' academic success. Several studies (Carrier et al., 1988; Kiewra, Benton, Kim, Risch, & Christensen, 1995; Kiewra et al., 1991a; Kiewra, Mayer, Christensen, Kim, & Risch, 1991b; Palmatier & Bennett, 1974; Rickards & Friedman, 1978) demonstrate that notetaking generally results in better student performance. The consistency of these findings leaves little doubt that improving the notetaking effectiveness for students should be a central objective for applied instructional communication research.

> "et al." is Latin for "and all."

> When two or more citations from the same author have the same year of publication, you must include lowercase letters (e.g., "a" and "b") to distinguish between the citations. Notice how this is used in the two Kiewra (1991) citations. In the list of references, alphabetize by author's last name to determine which citation is designated "a," which is "b," and so on.

Based on the rationale that notetaking effectiveness, and consequently achievement, is influenced by the way lecture information is presented, the present study explored whether or not the use of explicit organizational cues in a lecture could increase students' notetaking effectiveness and achievement. The study consisted of a 2 x 2 experimental design where students either took notes or did not take notes over a lecture containing or not containing organizational cues. It was hypothesized that students taking notes over the lecture containing organizational cues would achieve at higher levels on recall tests and that students hearing the lecture with organizational cues would take qualitatively and quantitatively more effective notes.

Review of Literature

Research exploring the importance of notetaking has found that both the quantity and quality of students' notes are important in terms of achievement. For example, Locke (1977) found that the number of ideas recorded in students' notes is positively related to recall of lecture information. Although the importance of recording a complete set of notes is intuitive, other aspects of notetaking (i.e., notetaking format) could also impact achievement. For instance, Kiewra and colleagues (1991a) found that using a matrix for notetaking was superior to conventional notetaking for immediate recall, and in another study, found that outline notetaking was superior to conventional notetaking in terms of both immediate and delayed recall (Kiewra et al., 1995). Evidence from other researchers indicates that notetaking combined with periodic summarization of main points from a lecture also boosts recall (Davis & Hult, 1997). Collectively, evidence on notetaking effectiveness leads to the conclusion that both the number of ideas recorded in students' notes (quantitative effectiveness) as well as the format of those ideas (qualitative effectiveness) are important elements of overall notetaking effectiveness and subsequent recall of information.

Given that notetaking effectiveness, both qualitative and quantitative, appears to impact achievement, how can teachers help students take better notes? Unfortunately, research in instructional communication provides little guidance in this area. Researchers in allied disciplines attempting to answer this question have explored various cuing techniques used during lecture situations that increase the quantity and quality of students' notes (for a review see Kiewra, 1991). For example, selection cues are strategies that help students pick out important elements from a lecture.

For most student papers you will use two types of headings: level 1 and level 2. Level 1 headings are centered in the page. Level 2 headings are flush to the left margin and italic. Use upper- and lowercase letters for all headings. Do not use boldface. "Review of Literature" is a level 1 heading.

APA style does not recommend for text features like bolding and italics. To emphasize text you should simply underline it.

Selection cues have been operationalized as conspicuous red or green cards to signal when notes should be recorded (Moore, 1968), writing information on the chalkboard (Locke, 1977) or providing other written signals (Frank, Garlinger, & Kiewra, 1989), use of skeletal outlines (Stencel, 1998), repetition of lectures (Kiewra et al., 1991b), and verbally stressing points by saying this is important (Scerbo, Warm, Dember, & Grasha, 1992). Each of the aforementioned selection cue strategies has been shown to increase the number of ideas recorded in students' notes.

Despite evidence that a variety of selection cues boost quantitative notetaking effectiveness, two salient questions remain unresolved. First, do these communication strategies increase the qualitative effectiveness of notes? Although the sheer quantity of ideas recorded in students' notes is undoubtedly related to achievement, the quality of those notes is also important. Currently, it is unclear whether or not cues used during a lecture have an effect on the qualitative effectiveness of notes. Second, at least some of the selection cues explored in previous research lack practical utility. Not all students have access to tapes of lectures, and consequently, repetition is not an option. Moreover, it is unlikely that many teachers will enthusiastically adopt the red card/green card strategy. Although we do not discount the utility of using importance cues, the chalkboard, or skeletal notes, our objective was to explore the utility of using another type of selection cue called organizational cues.

Organizational cues are verbal statements used by teachers to indicate the structural elements of a lecture. Such cues can include advance organizers, internal previews, internal summaries, and spoken numeric signposts of main and subordinate points. Although the effects of organizational cues in lectures have not been explicitly explored, two distinct programs of research suggest that these types of cues might improve students' notetaking and achievement.

Instructional communication researchers have consistently documented a connection between teacher immediacy and student learning. Although various theories have been used to explain this relationship, Kelley and Gorham (1988) speculate that immediacy cues increase students' attention to material. Although immediacy cues are distinct from organizational cues, Kelly and Gorham's rationale lends credibility to the argument that cues used during a lecture influence students' attention and learning. Other research in communication has found that the organization of information is also positively related to recall (Spicer & Bassett, 1976).

Although research in communication leads one to the conclusion that how teachers present information matters, research on cues used in expository text provides even more compelling evidence for the utility of organizational lecture cues. As explained by Lorch (1989), expository text includes a number of selection cues that signal readers about structural and content elements. Headings, titles, enumeration devices (e.g., numbering the points in an argument), and typographical characteristics are all examples of selection cues, or signals, found in text. Studies have found that organizational cues in text passages increase recall (Kardash & Noel, 2000; Myers, Pezdek, & Coulson, 1973), increase the quality of problem-solving solutions (Lockitch & Mayer, 1983), and decrease reliance on verbatim memory and primacy memory (Mayer, Cook, & Dyck, 1984). Although text signals boost achievement, questions remain whether these types of cues have a similar effect during lectures.

Based on the rationale provided in notetaking literature as well as literature on text signaling, several predictions were generated. First, previous research indicates that the cues provided during a lecture as well as student notetaking over a lecture improve student achievement. Consequently, it was predicted that students who took notes over the lecture containing organizational cues would learn more than students hearing lectures without cues and/or notetaking.

H1: Students who take notes over lectures containing organizational cues will score higher on achievement tests than students who do not take notes or hear lectures without organizational cues.

Furthermore, use of organizational cues could result in more effective notetaking because the cues make the organization of the lecture explicit. Thus, it was predicted that both the quantity and quality of students' notes would be greater in the cued condition than the uncued condition.

H2: Students who hear lectures with organizational cues will have qualitatively and quantitatively more effective notes than students who hear lectures without organizational cues.

Finally, previous research indicated that the completeness of students' notes is positively related to achievement. Because the organization of students' notes also potentially impacts their ability to store, organize, and retrieve information, it was predicted that both note completeness and note organization would be positively related to achievement.

H3: Student achievement is positively related to both note quantity and note organization.

> Double-space text throughout the manuscript.

Method

Participants & Design

Participants were 60 undergraduate students enrolled in a basic communication course at a large Midwestern public university. The basic communication course is required for most majors at the university; thus, participants were selected randomly from a potential sample representing a broad range of majors and academic backgrounds. There were slightly more females ($n = 31$) than males ($n = 27$; 2 did not report gender) and the participants' average age was 22.58 ($SD = 4.85$). In terms of class standing, 14 of the participants were Freshmen (23.3%), 11 were Sophomores (18.3%), 18 were Juniors (30%), and 17 were Seniors (28.3%). Participants indicated they had been in college for an average of 5.64 semesters ($SD = 3.35$) and had an average GPA of 2.95 ($SD = .52$). All participants received extra credit

for participation and were informed of their rights as participants with standard informed consent procedures. Participants were randomly assigned to one cell of a 2 x 2 design where the first factor was lecture cues (explicit organizational cues were either present or absent) and the second factor was notetaking (students either recorded lecture notes or listened without taking notes).

Experimental Materials

Materials used for the experiment included two versions of a scripted, audio-taped lecture as well as two tests to measure students' recall of lecture content. The lecture was read by a female colleague not involved in the experiment and was audio-taped to control for possible nonverbal communication effects. The lecture material addressed four different theories about human communication processes (Coordinated Management of Meaning, Universal Audience, General Systems theory, and Media Bias theory) by describing five common topic areas for each theory (definition/description, its predominant context, examples illustrating the theory, how the theory explains potential miscommunication, and a specific application of the theory).

Because the lecture was scripted and taped, two versions of the lecture were created: a cued and uncued version. The cued lecture contained explicit organizational cues which highlighted the structural organization of the lecture by drawing students' attention to the names and order of the theories and identified the five common topic areas. For example, the cued lecture contained these phrases: "The second context I will discuss is public communication," and "Now I will present a theory for public communication." Students in the cued lecture also heard an advance organizer in the introduction of the lecture. The advance organizer was worded in this way:

> This lesson describes four communication theories: coordinated management of meaning theory, universal audience theory, general systems theory, and media bias theory. For each of these theories, we consider five things: First, I will provide a description of the theory. Second, we discuss the communication context associated with the theory. Third, I will discuss how the theory helps us understand miscommunication in that context. Fourth, we will learn about an example of the theory. Finally, we consider how the theory can be applied to our understanding of communication.

The cued version of the lecture contained 3,045 words and lasted approximately 15 minutes.

Students hearing the uncued lecture heard the same information as students hearing the cued lecture; however, explicit organizational cues were omitted. For instance,

This is a block quotation of 40 words or more. Indent the entire quotation 1/2 inch or approximately five spaces from the left margin. Note that the quotation is double-spaced like the rest of the text.

information on Universal Audience theory was presented in
this way: "Another theory is Universal Audience theory which
can be described as. ..." Students hearing this lecture heard
the following statements rather than an advance organizer:

> In this lesson we consider several communication
> theories associated with several of the most common
> human communication contexts. To explain these, we
> will learn a lot of information, and after hearing it, you
> will have a much better understanding of what human
> communication is and how theories can help us
> understand how human communication works in a
> variety of situations and settings.

This version of the lecture contained 2,997 words and lasted
just over 13 minutes.

In addition to the lectures, two achievement tests were
constructed to assess students' recall from the lectures. The first
achievement test, called the structure test, asked students to
recall the lecture framework, including main topics (e.g., media
bias theory, coordinated management of meaning theory, etc.)
and subtopics (e.g., definition, example, application, etc.).
This test measured students' ability to recall and construct the
lecture's organization independent of specific facts or
examples. There were a possible 24 points on this test. The
second test, called the detail test, presented the organizational
framework of the lecture and asked students to provide
associated details. For example, students were asked to write
the definition, associated context, example, explanation of
miscommunication, and application for general systems theory.
This test assessed students' ability to recall specific facts and
details from the lecture relative to their superordinate topics.
Because there were five subtopics covered for each theory,
there were 20 possible points on this test.

Experimental Procedure

Students were randomly assigned to one of four rooms representing either the cued or uncued and either the notes or no-notes conditions. All students were provided verbal instructions that they would listen to and be quizzed over a lecture on communication theory. After listening to the lecture, all participants were given five minutes to review the information. Students in the notes condition were instructed to review their notes but were asked to put them away after the review period. Students in the no-notes condition were told to mentally review the information they had heard. After the review period, all participants were administered the two achievement tests and were instructed that they could not look ahead or backwards in the test packet, nor could they go back and change answers. All students completed the tests in 15 minutes or less. The experimental procedure including listening to the lecture, reviewing the information, and taking the tests lasted approximately 45 minutes.

Scoring and Analysis

Scoring of the achievement tests involved awarding one point for each structural element (structure test) and detail (detail test) recorded by students. In addition to analyzing students' achievement on the two tests, students' notes were analyzed for organization and completeness. Students' note organization was assessed by determining whether the names of the four communication theories and five corresponding categories (per theory) were present in notes. Thus, note organization scores could range from 0 to 24. Students' note completeness was assessed by counting the number of details contained in notes. The scores recorded for note completeness could range from 0 to 20.

After constructing a scoring/coding manual for the tests and students' notes, one of the researchers and a colleague not involved in the study independently scored five sets of materials. After this initial scoring session, the two compared their scores for the materials and discussed differences so that reliability on subsequent scoring could be increased. This procedure resulted in overall reliability estimates of .93 for the structure test, .96 for the detail test, .90 for note organization, and .87 for note details. The scores from the two coders were averaged so that each student had one score for each of the tests and measures of notetaking effectiveness.

Data were analyzed using SPSS for Windows; alpha was set at .05 for all statistical tests. To protect from type I error, a multivariate analysis of variance procedure was used to test for mean differences among treatment groups on each of the achievement tests. Univariate t-tests were used to test for mean differences in note completeness and organization based on the organizational cues factor. Finally, regression procedures were used to determine how much variance in students' scores on the three achievement tests could be accounted for by the teachers' use of organizational cues, note organization, and note completeness.

Results

Results of the statistical tests supported the predictions guiding the study. Students who heard the lectures with organizational cues scored higher on the achievement tests than students who heard the lecture without cues. The combination of taking notes over the cued lectures resulted in the highest achievement levels whereas not taking notes and hearing the uncued lecture resulted in the lowest. Moreover, students who heard the lectures with cues recorded more structural elements and details from the lectures in their notes than their peers who heard the lectures without cues.

Achievement Tests

Multivariate analysis of variance procedures was used to test for mean differences between each of the four groups in terms of scores on each of the two achievement tests. The multivariate tests showed significant main effects for both the notetaking factor, Wilks'λ = .79, F = 7.32 (2, 55), $p. < .05$, η^2 = .21, and the cues factor, Wilks'λ = .73, F = 9.10 (2, 54), $p. < .05$, η^2 = .27. A significant Cues x Notes interaction was also detected, Wilks'λ = .47, F = 31.35 (2, 55), $p. < .05$, η^2 = .53.

With respect to the structure test, including explicit organizational cues in the lecture and having students take notes, each resulted in higher scores. Significant main effects were found for both cuing, F = 52.17 (1, 56), $p. < .05$, η^2 = .48, and notetaking, F = 5.06 (1, 56), $p. < .05$, η^2 = .08. The interaction between cues and notetaking was not significant, F = 1.99 (1, 56), $p. > .05$, η^2 = .03. In terms of the detail test, a combination of notetaking and lecture cuing resulted in higher scores for students. Conversely, absence of cuing and/or notetaking resulted in substantially lower scores on this test. As with the lecture organization test, significant main effects were found for both cuing, F = 20.96 (1, 56), $p. < .05$, η^2 = .27, and notetaking, F = 12.03 (1, 56), $p. < .05$, η^2 = .18. Organizational cues and notetaking accounted for 27% and 18% of the variance in students' ability to recall lecture details, respectively. There was also a significant interaction between notetaking and cues for the detail test, F = 15.70 (1, 56), $p. < .05$, η^2 = .22. As indicated by comparisons of simple effects, students who heard the lecture with explicit organizational cues and took notes scored significantly higher on this test than students who did not take notes or who took notes and heard the uncued lecture. Thus, the combination of cuing and notetaking resulted in higher achievement.

Notetaking

Initially, correlations were calculated to determine the statistical relationships between students' notetaking and achievement. In general, correlations revealed significant and positive relationships between the two measures of notetaking effectiveness and students' scores on the two achievement tests. As indicated by the coefficients, both the quantity and quality of students' notes are strongly correlated with achievement. To further explore these relationships, regression analyses were calculated for each test with note organization, note completeness, and use of organizational cues entered as predictor variables. Because results of the ANOVA procedures suggested that organizational cues should account for significant variance in students' scores, this factor was entered first and students' note completeness and organization was entered in a second block. The combination of all three predictor variables accounted for 54% of the variance in students' scores on the organization test, and 59% of the variance on the details test. As indicated by the coefficients, use of organizational cues was the only significant predictor of students' scores on the organization test, and the organization of students' notes was the only significant predictor of scores on the detail test.

Students' notes were also analyzed to determine whether there were significant differences in students' note organization and note completeness depending on whether they heard the lecture with or without organizational cues. In general, the use of cues dramatically improved students' notes. Not only did students hearing the lecture with organizational cues record more structural elements of the lecture, but they also recorded more details. Tests of mean differences indicated significant differences for note organization, $t = 6.36$, $p < .05$, and note completeness, $t = 6.30$, $p < .05$. Students hearing the lecture with organizational cues recorded 54% ($M = 12.89$; $SD = 5.13$) of the organizational points and 64% ($M = 12.78$; $SD = 3.69$) of the lecture details, whereas students hearing the lecture not containing cues recorded only 15% ($M = 3.58$; $SD = 2.70$) of the organizational points and 29% ($M = 5.87$; $SD = 2.20$) of the lecture details, respectively. In practical terms, students hearing the lecture containing explicit cues recorded nearly four times as many structural points and over twice as many details as students hearing the lecture without these explicit cues.

Discussion

The purpose of this study was to assess the effectiveness of using organizational lecture cues to increase students' quantitative notetaking effectiveness, qualitative notetaking effectiveness, and achievement. It was predicted that students taking notes over the lecture with organizational cues would score higher on the achievement tests than students not taking notes or not hearing the lecture with cues. It was also predicted that students' notes in the cued lectures would contain more details and would be more organized than students' notes in the uncued lecture. Results of the study supported both of these predictions.

Based upon results of the experiment, three major findings are discussed. First, this study reconfirmed the previous finding that notetaking is strongly related to achievement (see Kiewra, 1984; Kiewra et al., 1995; Locke, 1977). In addition to the importance of note quantity, this study yielded new information concerning the importance of note quality as assessed through organization. Results indicated that when students recorded the organization of a lecture in their notes, they were more likely to remember specific details from the lecture. Although previous literature has documented the relationship between note completeness and achievement (see Locke, 1977), findings of the current study suggest that recording structural elements of a lecture is perhaps more important. Notably, the organization of students' notes was the only significant predictor of students' recall on the detail test.

Second, this study found strong support for the use of organizational lecture cues because of the impact they had on student notetaking and achievement. Students hearing lectures with organizational cues recorded twice as many lecture details and nearly four times as many organizational points as those students hearing the lecture without organizational cues. The importance of this finding is underscored when placed in the context of the previous finding: When teachers use organizational cues in lectures students record more organized notes, and when students record organized notes their achievement dramatically increases. In practical terms, one would expect that students will learn a great deal more when teachers use organizational cues when presenting material. In fact, this was demonstrated on the achievement tests where organizational cues had effect sizes of .48 for the structure test and .27 for the detail test, respectively.

The final finding of this study related to a potential interaction between a teacher's use of organizational lecture cues and student notetaking. Although a significant Cues x Notetaking interaction was found only on the detail test, this interaction pattern was consistent on the structure tests and a significant multivariate interaction was also observed. Moreover, power for the interaction term on the structure test was low (.23), which raises the possibility that a significant interaction would not have been detected. In short, students benefited most when they took notes and heard organizational lecture cues. Alternatively, students who did not take notes and/or did not hear organizational lecture cues performed more poorly. Consequently, we suggest teachers use organizational cues because this strategy is cheap, easy, and has a potentially dramatic impact on student learning.

Although this study has important pragmatic and theoretical implications, additional research is warranted. For instance, future research should explore the effects of organizational lecture cues in a more naturalistic setting. The audio-taped lectures used in this study, while useful for controlling confounding variables, may lack external generalizability. Moreover, additional research efforts should explore how these teaching and learning behaviors vary depending on whether the type of material being taught is declarative, procedural, or conceptual. For instance, would the importance of organizational clarity be magnified in situations where processes or behaviors are being taught? Finally, future studies should explore how organizational cues and notetaking impact learning among students with differing learning style preferences.

In conclusion, this study has explored the effects of teacher organizational clarity and student notetaking on cognitive learning. Results indicated that both teacher and student communication behaviors are critical elements in the classroom. In this study, students learned more when they took notes and when the teacher presented explicit organizational cues. It is advisable for teachers and students both to enact these behaviors because of their ease and the substantial effect they have on learning.

References

Carrier, C., Williams, M., & Dalagard, B. (1988). College students' perceptions of notetaking and their relationship to selected learner characteristics and course achievement. *Research in Higher Education, 28*, 223–239.

Davis, M., & Hult, R. (1997). Effects of writing summaries as a generative learning activity during notetaking. *Teaching of Psychology, 24*, 47–49.

Frank, B., Garlinger, D., & Kiewra, K. (1989). Use of embedded headings and intact outline with videotaped instruction. *Journal of Educational Research, 82*, 277–281.

Hartley, T., & Davies, I. (1978). Note-taking: A critical review. *Programmed Learning and Educational Technology, 15*, 207–224.

Kardash, C., & Noel, K. (2000). How organizational signals, need for cognition, and verbal ability affect text recall and recognition. *Contemporary Educational Psychology, 25*, 317–331.

Kelley, D., & Gorham, J. (1988). Effects of immediacy on recall of information. *Communication Education, 37*, 198–207.

Kiewra, K. (1984). Acquiring effective notetaking skills: An alternative to professional notetaking. *Journal of Reading, 27*, 299–301.

Kiewra, K. (1991). Aids to lecture learning. *Educational Psychologist, 26*, 37–53.

Kiewra, K., Benton, S., Kim, S., Risch, N., & Christensen, M. (1995). Effects of note-taking format and study technique on recall and relational performance. *Contemporary Educational Psychology, 20*, 172–187.

Observe the same margins and pagination requirements as the rest of the manuscript.

"References" is centered at the top of the page using upper- and lowercase letters. Double-space to the first entry.

List of references goes on a separate page.

Double-space after: "References," within each entry, and between each entry.

Kiewra, K., DuBois, N., Christian, D., McShane, A., Meyerhoffer, M., & Roskelley, D. (1991a). Note-taking functions and techniques. *Journal of Educational Psychology, 83*, 240–245.

Kiewra, K., Mayer, R., Christensen, M., Kim, S., & Risch, N. (1991b). Effects of repetition on recall and note-taking: Strategies for learning from lectures. *Journal of Educational Psychology, 83*, 120–123.

Locke, E. (1977). An empirical study of lecture note taking among college students. *The Journal of Educational Research, 77*, 93–99.

Lockitch, N., & Mayer, R. (1983). Signaling techniques that increase the understandability of expository prose. *Journal of Educational Psychology, 75*, 402–412.

Lorch, R. (1989). Text-signaling devices and their effects on reading and memory processes. *Educational Psychology Review, 1*, 209–234.

Mayer, R., Cook, L., & Dyck, J. (1984). Techniques that help readers build mental models from scientific text: Definitions pretraining and signaling. *Journal of Educational Psychology, 76*, 1089–1105.

McKeachie, W. (1999). *Teaching tips: Strategies, research, and theory for college and university teachers.* (10th ed.). New York: Houghton Mifflin Company.

Moore, J. (1968). Cuing for selective notetaking. *Journal of Experimental Education, 36*, 69–72.

Myers, J., Pezdek, K., & Coulson, D. (1973). Effect of prose organization upon free recall. *Journal of Educational Psychology, 65*, 313–320.

Palmatier, R., & Bennett, J. (1974). Notetaking habits of college students. *Journal of Reading, 18*, 215–218.

When lowercase letters are used in text citations to distinguish references, those letters must also appear in the reference citation. Notice the various Kiewra (1991) entries in this reference section. In the first entry no co-authors are listed and the years of publication are different. Consequently, no letter is needed. In the other entries the number of co-authors would result in the in-text citations appearing as "Kiewra et al., 1991." Lowercase letters are required to indicate which citation is being referenced. By alphabetizing authors' last names you can determine which citation should be designated as "a," "b," and so forth.

Rickards, J., & Friedman, F. (1978). The encoding versus the external storage hypothesis in note taking. *Contemporary Educational Psychology, 3*, 136–143.

Scerbo, M., Warm, J., Dember, W., & Grasha, A. (1992). The role of time and cuing in a college lecture. *Contemporary Educational Psychology, 17*, 312–328.

Spicer, C., & Bassett, R. (1976). The effect of organization on learning from an informative message. *The Southern Communication Journal, 41*, 290–299.

Stencel, J. (1998). An interactive lecture notebook: Twelve ways to improve students' grades. *Journal of College Science Teaching, 27*, 343–345.

APPENDIX E
Model Speaking Preparation Outline
Following APA Guidelines

Kip Johnson
Dr. Scott Titsworth
Speech 101
April 13, 2007

An Informative Speech on Cell Phones

Specific Purpose: To inform my audience about the advantages and disadvantages of cellular phones.

Central Idea: Cellular phones have several advantages and disadvantages as a mobile communication device, a health and safety tool, and a new opportunity for e-commerce.

Introduction

I. Think fast! You are working at your job and you start to go into labor. Or, imagine that you are driving home at night and your car stalls while it is below zero. Or, you are driving down the street and see a person being robbed on the sidewalk. What do you do? You could be like Keanu Reeves and take things into your own hands, or you could do what most sane people would do and make a call on your cell phone. But we have all probably witnessed the dark side of cell phones. While watching *Speed* in the theatre, your movie experience could likely be interrupted by a cell phone call to an inconsiderate moviegoer.

II. Cell phones are becoming an increasingly common element of our culture. Jorgen Bach, a professor from a university in Denmark, told *Time* magazine that an estimated 500 million people worldwide use cell phones, with 100 million of those being in the U.S. (Ressner, Sautter, Thomas, & Thompson, 2001).

III. I have owned a cell phone for nearly 2 years. Because I am worried about risks but also excited about the convenience of cell phones, I decided to investigate the benefits and risks of cell phones.

IV. I intend to inform you about cell phones so that you can make a decision on whether you would want one.
   A. In my speech I will inform you about the benefits and dangers of cell phones.
   B. I specifically address the following points:
      1. The benefits and risks of cell phones as a mobile communication device.
      2. The benefits and risks of cell phones for health.
      3. The benefits and risks of cell phones for e-commerce.

(Transition: We all know that the primary use of cell phones is for communication. In my first point I look at the uses of this communication tool as well as some dangers it poses.)

Single-space the text of the outline. Double-space between the major sections of the outline. This is done to conserve length.

Note that "Specific Purpose" and "Central Idea" are capitalized.

Introduction is a major section of the outline. Center, using upper- and lowercase letters. No bolding.

Many authors of public speaking texts allow you to write out the introduction and conclusion of the speech. Check with your instructor to see if this is an option for you.

Body ──────

> Center title of major section like "Body."

I. Cell phones are popular tools for mobile communication.

   A. Cell phones make communication easy and convenient.

      1. Personal example of working on a farm and using cell phones while in the field.

      2. Personal example of using my cell phone while driving to school.

      3. Approximately 85% of those who own cell phones use them while driving, according to the National Conference of State Legislators (National Conference of State Legislators, 1999).

> Start renumbering with Roman numeral "I" when you begin a new section of the outline.

   B. Although cell phones are convenient, they also pose a danger if not used properly.

      1. A study reported in the *New England Journal of Medicine* found that use of cell phones quadrupled the risk of an automobile accident (National Conference of State Legislators, 1999).

         a. This is equal to the impairment caused by legal intoxication.

         b. The use of hands-free devices does not appear to reduce the risk.

      2. Kaz Zielinski, a program manager for a company called Advanced Driver Training Services, explains that the act of using a cell phone simply distracts drivers (Zielinski, 2000).

         a. Dialing the phone causes you to look down.

         b. Talking on the phone can cause you to lose focus on objects, distance, etc.

         c. A ringing phone can startle you.

         d. Holding a phone reduces your ability to control the vehicle.

> Note the rule of twos. You can't divide an idea into one part. For every Roman numeral I there is a II; for every A there is a B; for every 1 there is a 2; for every a there is a b.

(Transition: Now that we know that cell phones are a convenient, but potentially dangerous communication device, let's explore the impact of cell phones on health.)

II. Cell phones are useful tools for health and safety, but pose some risks.

   A. Cell phones have benefits for health.

      1. Cell phones improve the response time in emergencies.

      2. Cell phones are used to help women.

         a. The Wireless Foundation home page (2001) describes a program where women at risk of domestic violence are given free cell phones with air time to stay in touch with their crisis counselors.

         b. To date, over 30,606 cell phones have been given out through this program.

> Transitional statements are written as complete sentences and appear in parentheses. Also note the double-spacing that sets off the transitional statement from the rest of the outline.

B. Even though cell phones help people, there is some question regarding potential health risks.
  1. Some studies show that the radiation from cell phones can be linked to brain cancer (Ressner et al., 2001).
  2. The evidence on this potential risk is not conclusive. A recent study in the *Journal of the American Medical Association* and another in the *New England Journal of Medicine* found no statistical link between cell phone use and cancer risk (Ressner et al., 2001).
  3. Cell phone companies are starting to indicate an SAR rating on cell phone literature. The rule of thumb is that a lower SAR rating (say around .22) is safer than a higher one (around 1.6).

(Transition: The final area we will look at is the use of cell phones in e-commerce.)

III. Cell phones are becoming an important tool for e-commerce.
  A. We know that cell phones make business more convenient.
    1. Business executives use cell phones to make calling convenient.
    2. Consumers are increasingly using cell phones.
      a. Cell phones are already used for basic e-commerce like purchasing news and information services, checking current stock prices, and purchasing simple things like tickets (Bethoney, 2001).
      b. A news article in the *E-Commerce Times* also noted that corporations like Microsoft and RealNetworks will soon start selling multimedia content like movies and videos that can be played on new-generation multimedia capable cell phones (Hillebrand, 2000).
  B. Although cell phones will undoubtedly become an important tool for e-commerce, there is some danger depending on what the tool is used for.
    1. A recent article in *Time* indicated that cell phones could be used to gamble (Schenker, 2001).
      a. Predictions estimate that online gambling will jump from $3 billion in 2000 to $58 billion by 2004.
      b. A global poll by a Swedish mobile phone maker found that cell phones will make the betting impulse easier.
    2. Using cell phones for gambling is just like throwing money away at the casino, only easier.

Conclusion

(Transition: Now that you have learned about some benefits and dangers of cell phones, I hope you can make an informed choice on whether to get one.)

I.   In this speech I have presented you with several facts and examples of how cell phones are good and bad.
  A. Cell phones are excellent mobile communication tools, but they pose a danger for drivers.
  B. Cell phones make us safer in emergencies, but some claim they might expose us to dangerous radiation.
  C. Cell phones are new tools for e-commerce, but they also might make it easier to lose money on impulse decisions to buy or gamble.
II. If you are driving around town and see a robbery taking place, using a cell phone is probably the best thing you could do. But, during those other times when life is not so exciting, keep in mind the dangers of using your cell phone.

References

Bethoney, H. (2001, January 15). Let your cell phone do the e-shopping. [Electronic version.] *eWeek*, p. 75. Retrieved from Expanded Academic Index database.

Hillebrand, M. (2000, June 29). Internet video head for cell phones. [Online exclusive.] *E-Commerce Times*. Retrieved from http://ecommercetimes.com

National Conference of State Legislators. (1999). Do any states restrict the use of cell phones in motor vehicles? *State Legislatures, 25*, 2.

Ressner, J., Sautter, U., Thomas, C., & Thompson, D. (2001, January 22). Buzzing about safety: The latest studies say there is no cell phone risk, but many users are making their own decisions about taking precautions. *Time*, pp. 48-52.

Schenker, J. L. (2001, January 22). Place your mobile bets: Gambling could be the killer application that will make third-generation cell phone licenses pay off. *Time*, pp. 46-48.

The Wireless Foundation (2001). Call to protect home page. In The Wireless Foundation home page. Retrieved from http://www.wirelessfoundation.org

Zielinski, K. (2000). Cell phones and driving: A dangerous mix? *Risk & Insurance, 11*, 17-18. Retrieved from Expanded Academic Index database.

Observe the same margins and pagination requirements as the rest of the manuscript.

"References" is centered at the top of the page using upper- and lowercase letters. Double-space to the first entry.

Include retrieval date only if information is not final.

If URL is given, delete database name, except for hard-to-find books and other documents of limited circulation.

Note no period at end of URL.

Note the hanging indent of 1/2 inch or five spaces.

List of references goes on a separate page.

Double-space after "References," within each entry, and between each entry.

With the exception of http:// all slashes and other punctuation are placed *after* the line break

APPENDIX F
Model Paper Following MLA Guidelines

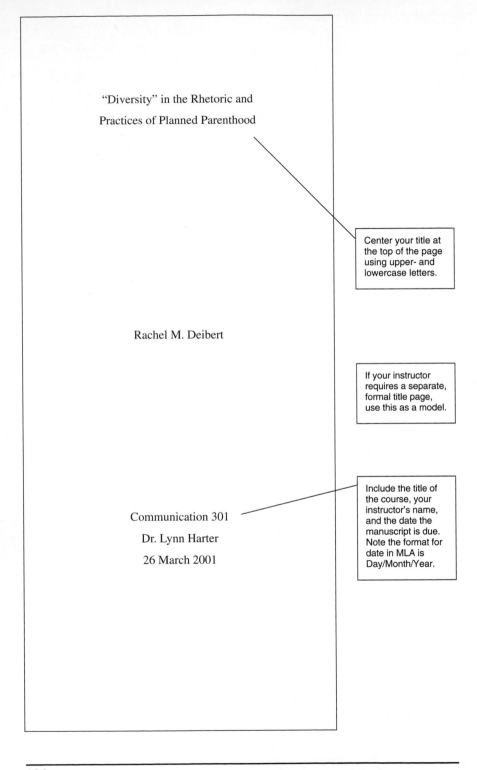

"Diversity" in the Rhetoric and
Practices of Planned Parenthood

Rachel M. Deibert

Communication 301
Dr. Lynn Harter
26 March 2001

Center your title at
the top of the page
using upper- and
lowercase letters.

If your instructor
requires a separate,
formal title page,
use this as a model.

Include the title of
the course, your
instructor's name,
and the date the
manuscript is due.
Note the format for
date in MLA is
Day/Month/Year.

"Diversity" in the Rhetoric and

Practices of Planned Parenthood

In organizational settings, "diversity" is a term often used in reference to people of different races, sexes, economic standings, sexual orientations, levels of physical and mental abilities, ages, and religions. Communication scholars often embrace a social constructionist perspective that recognizes notions of diversity as created and maintained through discursive interactions (e.g., Allen 143). In other words, our societal understandings of "diversity" emerge from how we talk about and enact, through a variety of practices, diversity. In this essay, I explore the rhetoric and practices of Planned Parenthood, an institution that has attempted to create an organizational culture that accepts and appreciates diversity. While Planned Parenthood seeks to provide reproductive care to a "diverse" clientele, upon closer examination the organization's practices fall short of its rhetorical vision and potentially disempower diverse populations.

Margaret Sanger established Planned Parenthood in 1916. Sanger was a leading activist in the early 1900s for women's reproductive rights. She maintained that women should have full control over their reproductive health, that every child should be wanted, and that sex should be pleasurable for both men and women. Despite jail time and public scrutiny, the Web page for Planned Parenthood explains that Sanger was a driving force in the legalization of birth control and other forms of contraceptives. Planned Parenthood has evolved into an organization whose "mission" is to provide a number of reproductive-related health services including pregnancy counseling, screening for sexually transmitted diseases, and contraceptive prescriptions, while creating an environment that values and respects "diversity."

If your instructor requires a separate title page, repeat the title of the paper centered at the top of the first page using upper- and lowercase letters.

Indent the first word of each paragraph of the manuscript 1/2 inch or approximately five spaces.

"e.g." is an abbreviation for the Latin phrase, *exempli gratia* (for example).

Do not justify the text; use a ragged right-hand margin.

Observe 1 inch margins top, bottom, left, and right.

Mission statements are one way that leaders attempt to cultivate both an "identity" and an "image" for organizations (Fairhurst, Monroe and Neuwirth 245). Mission statements articulate core values and principles that presumably guide members' choices and behaviors. Mission statements are "the corporate version of an ego ideal, a standard by which the corporation is supposed to measure itself" (Fairhurst, Jordan and Neuwirth 246). Mission statements are an increasingly popular form of corporate communication and are often expressed to both internal and external audiences. By expressing a formal ideology or belief system of the organization, mission statements ideally function to create "identification" between members, clients, and the organization (Cheney 360).

In its mission statement, Planned Parenthood creates an image of an organization that embraces diversity. "Planned Parenthood believes in the fundamental right of each individual, throughout the world, to manage his or her fertility. We believe that respect and value for diversity in all aspects of our organization are essential to our well being" (Planned Parenthood home page). While Planned Parenthood's mission statement is strategically ambiguous (Eisenberg 229), it does set a standard from which to judge its practices—a standard valuing "diversity." If we are to assume that Planned Parenthood's mission statement is a vision for organizational decision-making and practices of the organization, we would expect to find practices and discourse that target diverse individuals and their reproductive needs.

Planned Parenthood's mission is very vague in terms of how the organization "respects" and "values" diversity. In fact, it is unclear if and how care is provided to diverse individuals (e.g., men and women). Current programs, advertisements, and literature provided by Planned Parenthood better illustrate the amount of care diverse individuals are granted. While the programs of Planned Parenthood do feature elements consistent with their mission statement, care is largely provided to women. Pregnancy counseling is provided to women in the comfort of a doctor's office. Counseling for fathers of unwanted pregnancies or even wanted pregnancies is not provided. Planned Parenthood also serves as a leader of women's rights legislation and has supported bills and laws that exclude men from pregnancy decisions.

Trace evidence available in popular culture also illustrates how Planned Parenthood targets primarily women in marketing its services. One of the most current advertisements of Planned Parenthood focuses on the distribution of Emergency Contraception. Emergency Contraception, also known as The Morning After Pill, has become one of the most controversial drugs of the decade. Planned Parenthood has provided aid for women to obtain the drug. The advertisement features models and actress Stacy Dash (Clueless) scantily clad with the phrase, "Accidents happen . . . If you have unprotected sex. You have 72 hours to reduce your risk of getting pregnant" (Planned Parenthood home page). Other literature that Planned Parenthood distributes clearly targets females. Throughout its literature they use hypothetical examples that ignore the male voice in reproductive-related scenarios. Rather, the discourse emphasizes the internal monologue of women in hypothetical situations.

Planned Parenthood was established at a time when women received little rights and choices in carrying children and other reproductive matters. The organization was successful in its original mission to empower women. However, the formal rhetoric (i.e., the mission statement) of the organization

has evolved. The mission statement suggests that the

organization's "well-being" is dependent upon valuing and

respecting diversity. Yet, the practices and other discourse of

the organization appear to contradict this mission. In fact,

through its discourse Planned Parenthood potentially

undermines the importance of men in their organization and

their role in reproductive decision-making.

  Collectively, the discourse of Planned Parenthood

perpetuates the image that men are not to be held responsible

for reproductive decisions. This reflects and perpetuates

contemporary ideologies that place the responsibility of

protected sex, adoption, abortion, and other such decisions

exclusively on the shoulders of women. This ideology

potentially creates an organizational environment that does

not, in fact, value diversity in the form of welcoming men.

In this sense, Planned Parenthood falls short of its current

mission.

  What is even more dangerous is the lack of information

on men's health issues. Planned Parenthood does provide

screening for sexually transmitted diseases for both sexes

and distributes condoms. However, Planned Parenthood does

little else to value and respect the reproductive needs and

responsibilities of men. Nor does the discourse of Planned

Parenthood recognize men as active agents in reproductive

decision-making. It should come as no surprise that few men

regard Planned Parenthood to be a source of information on

their reproductive health. The clientele of Planned

Parenthood is typically composed of women without health

insurance or those interested in the privacy that the

organization provides (Planned Parenthood home page).

Without yearly examinations, men are at a greater

"i.e." is an abbreviation for the Latin phrase, *id est* (that is).

risk of developing irreversible health problems. If men do not receive proper screening, they can easily spread sexually transmitted diseases to their partners and the unborn. If men are not included in counseling sessions about reproductive decisions, they may be less likely to be committed to such decisions.

Underscoring existing literature about organizational mission statements is the acknowledged widespread failure in its implementation (Fairhurst, Jordan, and Neuwirth 244). Clearly, the case of Planned Parenthood illustrates this argument. While the organization formally recognizes that its well-being depends on valuing diversity, its practices contradict this mission. Perhaps the leaders of Planned Parenthood could argue that its goal is not to serve men; rather, its goal is to empower women. If that is the case, the organization should re-evaluate its mission statement. If the organization truly does intend to address the responsibilities and roles of diverse individuals (i.e., men and women) in reproductive health care, it should re-evaluate its discourse and practices.

Works Cited

Allen, Brenda. "Diversity and Organizational
Communication." <u>Journal of Applied Communication</u> 23
(1995): 143-55.

Cheney, George. "On the Various and Changing Meanings of
Organizational Membership: A Field Study of
Organizational Identification." <u>Communication
Monographs</u> 50 (1983): 342-62.

Eisenberg, Erik. "Ambiguity as Strategy in Organizational
Communication." <u>Communication Monographs</u> 51
(1984): 227-42.

Fairhurst, Gail, Jerry Jordan, and Kurt Neuwirth. "Why Are
We Here? Managing the Meaning of an Organizational
Mission Statement." <u>Journal of Applied Communication
Research</u> 25 (1997): 243-63.

Planned Parenthood home page. Planned Parenthood
Federation of America, Inc. 20 March 2001
<http://www.plannedparenthood.org/>.

The Works Cited is a separate page of the manuscript.

"Works Cited" is centered at the top of the page using upper- and lowercase letters. Double-space to the first entry.

Observe the same margins and pagination requirements as the rest of the manuscript.

The first line of each entry is flush with the left margin; subsequent lines are indented 1/2 inch or approximately five spaces.

APPENDIX G
Model Speaking Preparation Outline
Following MLA Guidelines

Mary Jane　　　　　　　　　　　　　　　　　Jane 1
Ms. Sandra House
Public Speaking 115
18 November 2002

Purchasing a Thanksgiving Turkey

Specific Purpose: To inform my audience of the factors to
consider when purchasing a Thanksgiving turkey.

Central Idea: When selecting a Thanksgiving turkey, the
informed consumer should consider four factors: the size, the
grade, the age, and whether the turkey is fresh or frozen.

Introduction

I.　How many of you are planning on having *Meleagris
gallopavo* for dinner in eight days? Well, this month on its
Thanksgiving homepage, Butterball predicted that not only
will ninety percent of all Americans enjoy a tasty meal of
Meleagris gallopavo next Thursday, all together, we will
consume a total of five hundred and thirty-five million
pounds of it. If you haven't guessed already, *Meleagris
gallopavo* is the scientific name for turkey.

II.　With so many of us honoring the three-hundred-year-old
tradition of turkey for Thanksgiving, it is important for us
to know the details we need to consider when we buy our
turkeys. These factors are the size of the turkey, the meat
grade of the turkey, the age of the turkey, and whether the
turkey is fresh or frozen.

Body

I.　Size is the most important factor to consider when
purchasing a turkey.
　A.　Buying the right size turkey is important because you
need enough to feed all your guests without having too
much left over.
　B.　Not everyone agrees on the formula you should use to
determine the size of turkey you want.
　　1.　On this month's Thanksgiving Web page, Norbest, the
world's third largest turkey company, says that you
should buy three-fourths pound per person.
　　2.　Butterball on its Web page suggests you calculate one
and one half pounds per person.
　　3.　However, honeysuckle white recommends one pound
per person.
　　4.　I would use one pound per person to figure the size
because it is easier.
　C.　The size is almost always written on the tag attached to
the neck of the bird.

Include your name,
instructor's name,
course number,
course title, and
date. Single-space
the head flush left.
Note the date
format in MLA is
Day/Month/Year.

Center the title of the
speech using
upper- and
lowercase letters.

Note that "Specific
Purpose" and
"Central Idea" are
capitalized.

Many authors of
public speaking texts
allow you to write
out your Introduction
and conclusion.

Single-space the
text of the outline.
Double-space
between the major
sections of the
outline: title, specific
purpose, central
idea statement,
introduction, body,
conclusion, and
transitional
statements. This is
done to conserve
space.

Note that the
indentation is
consistent
throughout at
1/2 inch. Also note
that all of the
symbols are aligned.
Main points A, B,
and C are aligned.
Subpoints 1, 2, 3,
and 4 are aligned.

The preparation
outline is written
in complete
sentences.

(Transition: After determining how large your Thanksgiving feast needs to be, the next major decision you need to make is the quality of the bird.)

II. What does the grade on the meat really mean?
   A. In their 1995 meat grading pamphlet, the Agriculture Marketing Service of the USDA says meat grading is a common language between producers and consumers.
   B. Grading is voluntary but according to the Nation Turkey Federation on its 1997 home page, seventy percent of all turkeys are USDA graded.
   C. The USDA assigns the letters A, B, and C to poultry meat depending on its quality.
      1. You should always buy Grade A meat.
      2. In 1995 the USDA reported that to be considered Grade A the meat must exhibit four things.
         a. It must have a normal shape and no missing parts.
         b. It must be free of all broken bones.
         c. It must have well-distributed fat.
         d. It must be free of all feathers and discoloration.
      3. The grade of the meat is always displayed somewhere on the packaging around the turkey.

(Transition: Once you know how large a turkey you need and what quality to look for, you need to know the age of the bird you are buying.)

III. You need to know the approximate age of the bird before you buy the turkey.
   A. Turkeys are classified as either old or young.
      1. Old birds are referred to as mature, yearling, or just old.
      2. Young birds are referred to as young or fryer-roaster.
   B. You should always buy young because it is more tender.

(Transition: The last major decision to make is whether you want to purchase a fresh or frozen bird.)

IV. Finally, you must decide whether you want a frozen or fresh turkey.
   A. The first thing to consider when deciding is how much preparation time you have.
      1. Fresh turkeys do not need to be thawed, but you shouldn't buy it too far in advance.
      2. Frozen turkeys can be bought months in advance, but need days to thaw.
   B. The second thing to consider is that fresh turkeys tend to be more tender.

Pagination appears on every page of the preparation outline. Pagination in MLA includes your last name, two spaces, and the page number 1/2 inch from the top and right margin.

Again, note the common system of indentation and symbol alignment throughout the outline.

Note the rule of twos. You can't divide an idea into one part. For every Roman numeral I there is a II; for every A there is a B; for every 1 there is a 2; for every a there is a b.

Transitional statements are written as complete sentences and appear in parentheses. Also note the double-spacing that sets off the transitional statement from the rest of the outline.

Conclusion ────────────────────────┐

Check with your
instructor to see if
you have the option
of writing out your
introduction and
conclusion.

Now you've heard enough on purchasing a Thanksgiving turkey
to make an informed decision about the turkey you want to buy,
whether it is a Butterball, Norbest, Honeysuckle white, or some
other brand of whole turkey. However, I advise you, next
Thursday when you are enjoying the time-honored tradition of
Melleagris gallopavo for Thanksgiving dinner, try not to think
of its size, grade, age, or whether it was frozen or fresh from the
store. Just enjoy the taste.

Jane   4

Works Cited ———

Butterball Turkey Company. "How to Prepare a Picture-

Perfect Turkey." <http://www.butterball.com>

(11 November 1999).

Honeysuckle white. "All about Turkey." <http://

www.honeysucklewhite.com/html/whole_turkey.html>

(11 November 1999).

The National Turkey Federation. "The Turkey Food Service

Manual." <http://www.turkeyfed.org/toc.html>

(16 November 1999).

Norbest Incorporated. "Talk'in Turkey Dinner." <http://

www.norbest.com> (11 November 1999).

United States Department of Agriculture. Agricultural

Marketing Service. "How to Buy Poultry." Washington,

D.C.: Government Printing Office, 1995.

United States Department of Agriculture. Agricultural

Marketing Service. "Meat Grinding and Certification

Service." Washington, D.C.: Government Printing Office,

1999.

The Works Cited is a separate page of the preparation outline as required by MLA.

"Works Cited" is centered at the top of the page using upper- and lowercase letters. Double-space to the first entry.

Observe the same margins and pagination requirements as the rest of the preparation outline—1/2 inch on all sides.

The first line of each entry is flush with the left margin; subsequent lines are indented 1/2 inch or approximately five spaces.

List the sources you cite in your preparation outline in alphabetical order following MLA guidelines for constructing a Works Cited page.

APPENDIX H
Student Exercises

Chapter 3 Exercise 1

Chapter 3 discussed several issues related to common written assignments in communication courses. Below are several terms and concepts from the chapter. For each term/concept, provide a brief definition/explanation based on what you read.

1. Full-Content Outline:

2. Speaking Outline:

3. Internal Source Reference:

4. Bibliographic Source Reference:

5. External Validity:

6. Internal Validity:

7. Negative Rationale:

8. Positive Rationale:

Chapter 3 Exercise 2

Based on information presented in Chapter 3, answer the following questions by writing the best answer in the space provided. For each question, write "T" for true or "F" for false. After indicating whether it is true or false, briefly explain why.

_____ 1. Internal source references for a full-content/preparation outline are included in the list of references or works cited.

_____ 2. Bibliographic references on a full-content/preparation outline are listed alphabetically.

_____ 3. Speaking outlines are typically two to four pages in length.

_____ 4. If the last point in your introduction is identified with the Roman numeral III, the first point in the body of your outline should be identified with the Roman numeral IV.

_____ 5. The Works Cited page (MLA) or References page (APA) for your outline should use Roman numerals to identify separate sources used in the outline.

_____ 6. Full-content/preparation outlines should be written using complete sentences.

_____ 7. Sub-subpoints (designated with regular numbers like "2") should be indented five spaces, or one tab, from the left margin of the outline.

Chapter 3 Exercise 3

Chapter 3 discussed several criteria that can be used to evaluate empirical and/or humanistic research studies. For each criterion below, provide a brief definition/explanation based on what you read.

Theoretical Scope:

Appropriateness of Methodology:

Validity:

Heuristic Value:

Parsimony:

Chapter 3 Exercise 4

Chapter 3 discusses how various writing assignments common in communication courses should be prepared. The section on composing a literature review suggests that literature reviews should be "mapped out" to determine how topics should be organized. For example, the research report included in Appendix D could be mapped using an inverted funnel as the visual representation of how it is organized. Using the model paper in Appendix A (APA version) or Appendix F (MLA version), construct a visual map of how that paper is organized. Use another page to draw your representation. To help you get started, begin by outlining the main points of the paper on the remainder of this page. You can then use that outline to help construct your visual map.

Chapter 4 Exercise 1

There are at least 10 citation errors in the following list of Works Cited. None of the errors involves spelling, grammar, or spacing. Circle each error in the following list and provide a correction. Turn the corrected list of Works Cited in to your professor as instructed.

Works Cited

Aldinger, C. "Pentagon Justifies Attack." <u>ABC News.com</u>. 1 Sept. 1999.
 <http://www.abcnews.go.com/go/sections/world/DailyNews/kosovo_
 main_990515.html>.

Bourhis, John. <jsb806f@mail.smsu.edu> <u>Updating the Style Manual</u>. Personal
 email. 1 June 1999. Sept. 29, 1999.

"Call It Cybernoia." Philadelphia Daily News, March 1, 1997, p. 11.

Harnack, Andrew, and Kleppinger, Eugene. <u>Online! A Reference Guide to Using</u>
 <u>Internet Sources</u>. New York: St. Martin's.

Johannesen, R. Ethics in Human Communication, 4th ed. Prospect Heights:
 Waveland Press, 1996.

Nichols, M. <u>The Lost Art of Listening</u>. Prentice-Hall, 1995.

Raymond, Kelly. Toward a New Tolerance: Gun Control and Community
 Policing. <u>Vital Speeches</u> 60 (1993): 332-334.

Wolvin, Andrew, and Carolyn Coakley. <u>Listening</u>, 6th ed. Dubuque: Brown and
 Benchmark, 1995. 223-396.

Chapter 4 Exercise 2

Based on the information presented in Chapter 1, answer the following questions by writing the best answer in the space provided. For each question, write "T" for true or "F" for false.

_____ 1. MLA stands for Modern Linguistic Association.

_____ 2. MLA style requires that you include a formal title page for every paper you submit for evaluation.

_____ 3. When using a direct quotation, MLA requires that you provide the reader with a page reference for locating the material quoted.

_____ 4. You should seriously consider justifying the right margin of your manuscript because it makes the manuscript look more professional.

_____ 5. It is generally a good idea to keep a photocopy of any written work you submit for evaluation for your personal files.

_____ 6. MLA style requires that you always double-space.

_____ 7. Proper pagination in MLA consists of your last name and the page number in the upper right-hand corner of the paper.

_____ 8. All scholarly writing submitted for evaluation requires pagination.

_____ 9. The first page of an MLA manuscript is the first page on which the text of the manuscript appears.

_____ 10. In MLA, the list of works cited appears at the end of the paper.

Your Name: _____ Date _____

Chapter 5 Exercise 1

There are at least 18 errors in the following list of references. Circle each error in the following list and provide a correction. Turn the corrected list of references in to your instructor.

REFERENCES

Adams, C. A. (1991). <u>Influences on the production and evaluation of regulative messages: Effects of social cognition, situational, and experiential variables in communication between hospital supervisors and volunteers</u>. Unpublished doctoral dissertation: University of Kansas.

Applegate, J. L. (1990). Constructs and communication: A pragmatic integration. In R. Neimeyer & G. Neimeyer (eds.), <u>Advances in personal construct psychology, Vol. 1</u> (pp. 197-224). Greenwich, CT: JAI.

Applegate, J. L., Burke, J. A., Burleson, B. R., Delia, J.G., and Kline, S. L. (1985). Reflection-enhancing parental communication. In I. E. Siegel (Ed.), <u>Personal belief systems: The psychological consequences for children</u> (pp. 107-142). Hillsdale, NJ: Erlbaum.

Bingham, S. G., & Burleson, B. R. (1988). Multiple effects of messages with multiple goals. <u>Human Communication Research, 16,</u> pp. 184-216.

Bonhoeffer, D. (1954). <u>Life Together</u> (J.W. Doberstein, Trans.). San Francisco: Harper San Francisco.

Burgoon, M. (1995). A Kinder, Gentler Discipline: Feeling Good About Being Mediocre. In B. Burelson (Ed.), <u>Communication yearbook 18</u> (pp. 464-479). Thousand Oaks, CA: Sage.

Burleson, B.R. (1989). The constructivist approach to person-centered communication: Analysis of a research exemplar. In Dervin, B, Grossberg, L, O'Keefe, B. & Wartellam E. (Eds.), <u>Rethinking Communication: Vol. 2. Paradigm Exemplars</u> (pp. 29-46). Newbury Park, CA: Sage.

Cheney, G. (1995). Democracy in the workplace: Theory and practice from the perspective of communication. <u>Journal of Applied Communication Research, 23,</u> 167-200.

Your Name: _____ Date _____

Chapter 5 Exercise 2

The following pages from a sample paper contain at least 10 errors in APA style. Circle each error and provide a correction. Turn the corrected pages in to your professor as instructed.

Running Head: Supervising Volunteers

SUPERVISING VOLUNTEERS:

INFLUENCES ON THE LOGIC OF MESSAGES DESIGNED TO REGULATE BEHAVIOR

Carey Adams

Southwest Missouri State University

Gregory J. Shepherd

University of Kansas

Supervising Volunteers:

Influences on the Logic of Messages Designed to Regulate Behavior

Volunteerism is an important facet of American society. From de Tocqueville's praise of the volunteer spirit of 19th century America to George Bush's "thousand points of light," volunteerism has been recognized as a virtue in American culture and has been repeatedly called upon in the service of individual and social needs. A recent survey estimated that 80 million American adults donated 19.5 billion hours of service through volunteer efforts in a single year (Ilsley, 1990). Hospitals have traditionally been among the institutions that rely most heavily upon the services of volunteers. Indeed, recent cuts in federal funding have forced social services to rely more heavily on volunteer efforts than ever before (Rosentraub), and hospitals have been steadily expanding their volunteer programs to extend volunteer responsibilities beyond distributing magazines, delivering flowers, and visiting patients (see, for example, the model programs detailed in Developing an older volunteer program, 1981).

The increasing demand for volunteer services in hospitals has led to concern about the retention of volunteer staff in such organizations. A growing body of research has examined questions of volunteer satisfaction (e.g., Paradis, 1987, Lee & Burden, 1990). Not surprisingly, Mausner has shown that the quality of a volunteer's experience is closely related to the quality of the relationship that volunteer enjoys with the supervisory staff of the organization (1988). And, given the wealth of research that has suggested the quality of communication in superior-subordinate relationships is a good predictor of job satisfaction generally (Downs & Hazen, 1976; Pincus, 1986; Clampitt & Downs, 1987; Clampitt & Girardi, 1987), it is not. . . .

Index